HOW TO FIND, HIRE AND KEEP THE RIGHT
DOMESTIC
PROFESSIONALS

Dear Mar,

Please enjoy!

JT. Kardwell

HOW TO FIND, HIRE AND KEEP THE RIGHT
DOMESTIC
PROFESSIONALS

The Household Employer's Guide
to Hiring Great Employees
Who Will Stay for Years

ALEKSANDRA KARDWELL

FIRST MANHATTAN PRESS

For more information, please email the author at:
akardwell@hamptonsemployment.com

Published by First Manhattan Press, a DBA of Hamptons Employment Agency, Inc. Hamptons Employment Agency's DCA License Number is 2079789-DCA.

For information about Hamptons Employment Agency, Inc., please visit:
www.hamptonsemployment.com

Research, composition, and editorial collaboration provided by Ross Kardwell.

ISBN 978-1-7336344-0-3

Printed in the United States of America

CONTENTS

INTRODUCTION

Dear Reader,

Firstly, I would like to thank you for taking time to read this book. Hiring the right domestic staff member can make a dramatic difference in your family's quality of life and peace of mind. But finding the right employee to work at your residence can be a time-consuming and challenging process. The goal of this book is to provide you with information that helps you significantly increase your chances of hiring someone great who will stay with you for years to come.

Throughout the book, I use the words domestic staff, household staff, residential staff, and private service staff interchangeably. For those unfamiliar with any of those terms, please be assured that I mean them all to describe the same thing — professional domestic staff. Moreover, because I expect the vast majority of readers of this guide to be based in the United States, the information contained herein is geared toward employers with residences in the U.S.

If you're wondering if this book is for you, I can tell you that it is if you fall into any of the following categories:

➤ You're a principal experienced with hiring domestic staff, but you would like to gain practical, cutting-edge information to make your next hire the best one possible.

➤ You're a principal who has not hired residential staff before, and you would like to learn about the process and techniques for making smart, lasting domestic hires.

➤ You're an estate manager, house manager, or personal assistant who's experienced with hiring domestic staff, and who's looking to hone your skills in evaluating, hiring, and keeping great staff members.

➤ You're a new (or relatively new) estate manager, house manager, or personal assistant tasked with making the right domestic staff selections for your employer.

➤ You're a residential real estate agent, builder, or other member of the real estate industry, and you're looking to learn more about the domestic staffing field.

➤ You're someone who doesn't fall into the categories above, but you're interested in learning more about the process for finding, hiring, and keeping the very best household employees.

Since 2011, I've worked with hundreds of clients located in areas such as New York City, The Hamptons, Long Island's Gold Coast, Greenwich, Boston, and Palm Beach. In that time, I've had the privilege to help a wide range of families and individuals. My clients have ranged from CEOs with ten-figure net worths, to Hollywood actors, to low-key individuals seeking peace, quiet, and a private lifestyle.

Over the years, I've learned a great deal about the needs of household employers, and I've gained an in-depth understanding of what works in domestic hiring. In *How to Find, Hire and Keep the Right Domestic Professionals: The Household Employer's Guide to Hiring Great Employees Who Will Stay for Years*, I'll share with you my experience, insights from thought leaders in the staffing field, and findings from the latest employment research. This practical, hands-on book is filled with timely information and actionable advice to help you identify, hire, and keep the right people for your unique needs and preferences.

Inside, you'll learn about the following topics:

◆ How to create a profile of the right person from the start of your search

◆ How to write job descriptions that attract great people

◆ Ways to recruit well-qualified candidates

- Powerful tips for reviewing resumes
- How to conduct effective interviews
- Using red flags and background checks to avoid hiring mistakes
- Tips for making job offers that candidates accept
- How to use a welcome letter to get everyone on the same page
- Steps to help new employees start work successfully
- How to keep great people for the long term
- Salaries and descriptions of domestic positions
- Legal considerations for avoiding employment problems
- Information on following tax requirements
- And much more

I sincerely hope that you gain much information that is valuable to you from this book. Should you have any questions, please feel free to contact me personally at:

Email: akardwell@hamptonsemployment.com
Phone: 631-204-1100

Enjoy the book!

Sincerely,

A. Kardwell

Aleksandra Kardwell
Southampton, NY

PART I.

HOW TO FIND GREAT DOMESTIC CANDIDATES

1. ETHICS – THE BEDROCK OF SUCCESSFUL MATCHING

The foundation of truly successful employer-employee matches is grounded in shared ethics. As in everything else, when it comes to domestic staffing, if you do good, good things will ultimately happen. *Like attracts like.* And employers who treat their household staff honorably — as valued individuals — often keep their people for a very long time.

To attract and keep the best people possible, it's of the utmost importance to operate in an honest and fair way. As I'll explain later, you'll have the best chance of finding a great employee for the position at hand by being straightforward about the realities of that position — the pros as well as the cons.

The domestic staffing community is small, and private employers, whether they have large or single-member staffs, develop reputations among household professionals. If a domestic employer wants ethical staff members but has not developed a good reputation, then it will be a challenge for that employer to hire great people. Talented, ethical employees will decide to work for employers whose ethics more closely match their own.

Of course, employers must also be careful to identify and select ethical candidates, as the reality is that some job seekers operate less than honorably (fortunately, unethical domestic professionals are the exception to the rule). Accordingly, as I'll discuss later, you must read between the lines when reviewing applicant resumes; conduct structured, thoughtful interviews; and ask the right questions when checking references to make sure that candidates are accurately presenting themselves. By digging deeper and asking questions that, when necessary, may make an applicant uncomfortable, you can gain a more accurate picture of the person behind the presentation. Those candidates who exaggerate, mislead, leave out key information, or otherwise misrepresent themselves should be quickly disqualified from your consideration.

After you've chosen a great employee, you'll keep that individual by making it clear what you expect of the person, treating them professionally and with respect, and rewarding your employee for good performance. While you have every right to expect superior performance from your household employee, "reciprocity" definitely applies: treat your staff as you would like to be treated. You'll have a positive, low- or no-drama household with minimal staff turnover.

> AFTER YOU'VE CHOSEN A GREAT EMPLOYEE, YOU'LL KEEP THAT INDIVIDUAL BY MAKING IT CLEAR WHAT YOU EXPECT OF THE PERSON, TREATING THEM PROFESSIONALLY AND WITH RESPECT, AND REWARDING YOUR EMPLOYEE FOR GOOD PERFORMANCE.

At Hamptons Employment Agency, Inc., an award-winning domestic staffing firm that I founded in 2011, we've always been concerned with creating excellent matches that last. Our success has, to a large degree, come from striving to make sure that we place great employees with great employers. While domestic positions can be highly demanding — it's the nature of the work — we're simply not interested in working with any employer looking to unfairly take advantage of their employees or vice versa. Our primary goal is to make lasting domestic matches beneficial for everyone concerned.

2. DEVELOPING A CLEAR PICTURE OF YOUR IDEAL EMPLOYEE

One of the most valuable things that you can do to find the right person for your unique needs and preferences is to carefully think through exactly what you're looking for at the very start of your employee search. This single factor — *clearly defining what you're looking for* — is, perhaps, the key element that leads to successful hiring.

As simple as it may sound, the failure to properly define what and who is needed is one of the leading causes of frustration, unnecessary expense, and failed employer-employee matches. If you take away nothing else from this guide but an understanding of the importance of being clear on your position's requirements and the type of person you want, then you will *massively* increase your chances of finding a great person who will stay with you for years to come.

For example, if you have a primary and a secondary residence, and you're looking to hire a House Manager who will travel to your secondary residence and work there seasonally on weekends, then you would want to find someone whose profile includes a willingness to travel between residences and a willingness to work on weekends. A House Manager with otherwise great experience but obligations or preferences that preclude travel and weekend work would not be a good fit for the position at hand. While this may seem like an obvious point, it is more common than one might think for details such as those just described to be improperly covered, especially during initial interviews.

CLEARLY DEFINING WHAT YOU'RE LOOKING FOR IS, PERHAPS, THE KEY ELEMENT THAT LEADS TO SUCCESSFUL HIRING.

KEY JOB-RELATED QUESTIONS TO ASK YOURSELF

So, what exactly should you do to get clear about who and what you need? *Hiring and Keeping the Best People* by Harvard Business School Press offers sound advice on what questions to ask yourself to successfully gain clarity. Since *Hiring and Keeping the Best People* is focused on business hiring, I've modified the questions to make them applicable for domestic hiring.

◆ What are the main responsibilities and tasks required for the job?

◆ What experience, skills, abilities, and education are necessary?

◆ Which personal characteristics are you seeking? Do you need someone who is hands-on, detail-oriented, classically trained, etc.?

◆ How would you characterize your household's culture? Is it formal or informal, structured or more open?

◆ What is your personal management style (e.g., authoritative, consultative, participative, etc.), and what sort of person would be able to work best in the job given that style?

THREE STRATEGIES TO HELP DETERMINE WHO'S RIGHT FOR YOU

The late business staffing expert Robert Half recommended a number of sound strategies in his book, *Robert Half on Hiring*, and I believe his ideas apply equally well to domestic hiring. You'll see me mention Mr. Half again in this book, as he was a giant in the staffing field and a pragmatic, enormously successful professional (today, the public company that bears his name generates over $5 billion in annual revenue).

Three of Mr. Half's most powerful strategies to help you determine who would be best-suited for your job are listed below.

1) Identify two or three characteristics that you believe are most essential to a candidate's ability to do

the job well. By determining in your mind the key characteristics required, you'll help yourself to stay focused on what's most important during the hiring process.

2) Identify two or three negative aspects of the job, and then think about what sort of individual could best handle them. Examples of what might be considered negative aspects (at least for some candidates) include a requirement for occasional night work; a requirement for six-day work weeks with long hours; and the need to travel to multiple residences throughout the year.

3) Think about past high-performers. If you were happy with the last person (or the last couple of people) in the position you're looking to fill, then it's a good idea to determine what, specifically, led to their good performance. Then, note these characteristics at the top of your requirements list. Of course, it's important to guard against trying to find a clone of a successful former employee; you may be left searching for a replacement for a long time.

SUPER PREDICTORS OF ON-THE-JOB SUCCESS

Assuming the candidates on your shortlist each have the core experience, skills, abilities, and intelligence required for the job at hand, what factors should you look at most closely to optimize your chances of making a great, long-term hire? With the myriad factors available for assessing candidates, wouldn't it be enormously valuable to know which ones you should think about most? Fortunately, current research can point us in the right direction.

Adam Robinson, CEO of Hireology, a firm which uses predictive data and other current technologies to help employers make smart hiring decisions, identifies four "Super Elements" for assessing candidates in his 2017 book, *The Best Team Wins*. These Super Elements are attitude, accountability, past-related job success, and cultural fit. If a candidate rates favorably on each of these four measures, you can expect there to be high odds that they will do well in the position at hand.

Let's take a closer look at each of these Super Elements below.

1) Attitude

Robinson defines attitude as an individual's overall disposition toward their work. A positive personality and a general feeling of satisfaction that persists across different prior work experiences is a key element to which you should give particular consideration. In short, look for upbeat individuals who gain real fulfillment from their work and who don't view their work as solely a means to make a living.

> A POSITIVE PERSONALITY AND A GENERAL FEELING OF SATISFACTION THAT PERSISTS ACROSS DIFFERENT PRIOR WORK EXPERIENCES IS A KEY ELEMENT TO WHICH YOU SHOULD GIVE PARTICULAR CONSIDERATION.

2) Accountability

This second element centers on the degree to which an individual believes that they have direct control over work-related outcomes. People who believe that they can help produce effective, positive outcomes, and who take responsibility for their mistakes, usually do better than those who have more of a victim-type mentality.

3) Past-Related Job Success

Most researchers generally agree that past behavior is the best predictor of future behavior. Interestingly, research done by Robinson and his team has found that 50% of the factors predicting a new employee's success or failure in a position have nothing whatsoever to do with that individual's experience. In looking at an applicant's experience, it's best to evaluate the extent to which the candidate met formal goals at previous jobs similar to the goals you have for the position at hand. If someone has proven that they can meet objectives close to the ones required of the position at hand, there's a good chance that the individual will succeed.

4) Cultural Fit

It's critical that a new employee has similar, shared values to those of your household. Household culture can be a bit of a gray area, but it makes sense to try to think about your household's core values before you meet with applicants. Whoever you hire must be able to work well in your particular environment and with the other individuals in the environment, including the principals and their family, managers, and other staff members. Sometimes candidates who may seem like superstars on the face of things would be better suited for employment elsewhere because the cultural fit is simply not there. Carefully consider how much authentic interest an applicant shows in your available position. Remember, similar values + real interest in the job = a high chance of job success.

I'd also like to point out that gaining clarity about who you want and need for your open position is an area where a seasoned professional at a leading domestic

> IF SOMEONE HAS PROVEN THAT THEY CAN MEET OBJECTIVES CLOSE TO THE ONES REQUIRED OF THE POSITION AT HAND, THERE'S A GOOD CHANCE THAT THE INDIVIDUAL WILL SUCCEED.

agency can add a lot of value for you. Experienced placement specialists have met with thousands of candidates, and they have helped hundreds or thousands of clients find good household help. Such specialists develop a strong feel for both candidates and clients and can thus assist with providing applicants who have not only the right experience, skills, and abilities, but also the right attitude, level of accountability, and cultural fit. By speaking with a specialist about your unique situation, you can gather suggestions about the type of domestic staff member who would likely be best suited to your needs.

Lastly, I believe that it's important to mention that prospective clients sometimes approach my firm, Hamptons Employment Agency, seeking one specific type of domestic worker; however, after one of my team members or I speak with the employer, it becomes evident that other options might suit the employer equally well or even better. For example, one client with whom I recently worked was initially committed to hiring only a live-in domestic couple. However, after learning more about the employer's situation, I suggested that they might also want to consider hiring a live-in house manager and a live-out housekeeper instead of hiring a couple. This additional option served to meet the client's needs while also expanding the pool of strong candidates.

3. HOW TO WRITE JOB DESCRIPTIONS THAT ATTRACT GREAT PEOPLE

With a clear picture of your ideal employee in mind, you can then create a compelling job description that attracts strong candidates who will likely do well at your residence. A job description is a concise yet comprehensive profile of your open position. It should contain all the essential information about the job, including the work schedule, duties, compensation, etc. I recommend using the following checklist for inclusion in each of your job descriptions.

JOB DESCRIPTION CHECKLIST

- ◆ Title
- ◆ Location
- ◆ Work schedule
- ◆ Residence type (e.g., formal, informal, etc.)
- ◆ Core responsibilities
- ◆ Other duties
- ◆ Skill requirements or preferences
- ◆ Experience requirements or preferences
- ◆ Personal characteristic requirements (e.g., "high-energy" or "hands-on")
- ◆ Education requirements or preferences (if applicable)
- ◆ Living arrangements (i.e., live-in or live-out)
- ◆ Travel requirements (if applicable)
- ◆ Salary range

To give you a clear idea of what your job description should look like, I have included a few samples. Feel free to adapt the following job descriptions to suit your needs. You'll notice that the headline for each position starts out with the type of staff member wanted. To quickly attract qualified applicants, it's good practice to start with, for example, the words "House Manager" and not "Full-Time, Live-In House Manager."

Example 1:

Domestic Couple: Full-Time, Live-In, Palo Alto — $150,000 to $180,000 per Year, Plus Benefits

Family in Palo Alto is seeking a full-time, live-in Domestic Couple for their residence. Duties include full housekeeping, laundry, household shopping, minor maintenance, cooking meals for the family, and providing formal serving for the meals. Pet care for one dog is also required. The schedule for this position is Monday through Friday, with occasional weekends required. At least three years of experience working together as a domestic couple is required. Starting salary for the position is $150,000 to $180,000 per year, plus full benefits.

Example 2:

Housekeeper: Full-Time, Year-Round, Live-In, Manhattan — $65,000 to $75,000 per Year, Plus Benefits (depending on experience)

Family of five is seeking a full-time, live-in Housekeeper for their home in New York City. The schedule for this position is Monday through Friday. Candidate responsibilities include full housekeeping, heavy laundry and ironing, occasional babysitting, and light cooking for the family's three children. You will share responsibilities with the family's other full-time Housekeeper. We're seeking a candidate with a quiet, hard-working disposition. You must have at least five years of experience working in a fine home. Salary will include full benefits for the right candidate.

Example 3:

Lead Butler: Full-Time, Year-Round, Southampton, NY — Up to $120,000 per Year, Plus Benefits

Family in Southampton is seeking a full-time, year-round Lead Butler. The right candidate must have at least five years of experience managing household staff and running a fine home. Candidate will oversee contacting and scheduling vendors and making staff and household schedules. You will prepare the estate for the family's arrival on weekends as well as for holidays, parties, and events. Duties will also include running miscellaneous errands and driving. The schedule is five days per week, to include weekends and holidays. Formal dining service experience is required, as you will be training all staff members in formal service.

You might find it helpful to have your job descriptions with you when you interview applicants. When you're in the midst of interviewing, it can sometimes be difficult to think about all the various aspects of the position for which a candidate must be a good fit. With your job description in hand, you can help stay focused on covering what's most important when you interview.

If you decide to work with a household staffing agency, having a comprehensive job description will also be highly valuable. By providing your staffing specialist with your job description, they will be able to develop a clear picture of your specific needs and preferences. This will allow the specialist to present you with candidates who nicely match your unique requirements.

> WHEN YOU'RE IN THE MIDST OF INTERVIEWING, IT CAN SOMETIMES BE DIFFICULT TO THINK ABOUT ALL THE VARIOUS ASPECTS OF THE POSITION.

Before finishing this chapter, I'd like to offer a simple and easy tip for attracting more qualified candidates to your position. Think through how many years of experience you really need for your position. For example, some employers will indicate that candidates must have five years of experience to apply. However, for many employers, strong candidates with three years of experience would likely do the job as well or better than some of the candidates with a longer work history. By lowering your years-of-experience threshold, you can easily attract a greater number of good applicants whom you would otherwise have lost right from the start.

In certain cases, requiring a high number of years of experience may event hurt a household employer. For example, a few years ago, I worked with a client's manager who was looking to hire a couple that had a minimum of five years of experience at one residence. The manager advised me that the client had very specific needs and selected a couple with ten years of experience. The client then trialed the highly experienced couple for a weekend. During the trial, the client was not fully satisfied and mentioned that the couple had their own style and habits from their past job — a fact that the client did not like.

I then urged the client's manager to consider a talented, eager-to-work couple who was relatively new to the domestic field (with only six months of experience as a couple). I advised the manager that because this particular couple was new to the field, they would be more open-minded and eager to do things the specific way that the client wanted things done. The manager was initially hesitant, but he then considered my advice, interviewed the couple, and decided to give them a try. The couple proved to be flexible, and they did a great job of doing things just the way the client wanted. As a result of the manager's and client's openness to trying the second, less experienced couple, the client found employees who did great work and who are still with the family today. It turned out to be an excellent match, beneficial for all involved.

4. FIVE WAYS TO RECRUIT THE BEST CANDIDATES FOR YOUR JOB

As you begin the process of working to recruit well-qualified domestic applicants, it's helpful to think about three core factors described by Robert Half in *Robert Half on Hiring*. These factors are listed below, and they will help you to determine the recruitment source that's best for you:

1) The nature of the job you're looking to fill,

2) How challenging you expect it to be to identify and attract strong candidates, and

3) How much time you can take to work on recruitment (for many employers, this is often the most important factor to consider).

For example, if you're seeking a new butler and, for whatever reason, you do not need to make a hiring decision for a few months and you have ample time available to recruit, then you may choose to use a number of options listed below (e.g., seeking referrals and running online and print ads). If, on the other hand, you need to fill a position quickly and your time is limited, then you might choose to run online ads and work with an agency. Giving thought to these issues upfront can help reduce stress and best set you up to fill the position at hand within your preferred time frame.

> A WELL-WRITTEN JOB DESCRIPTION WILL HELP YOUR HIRING MANAGER SUCCESSFULLY IDENTIFY AND SELECT SOMEONE WHO CAN EFFECTIVELY DO THE JOB.

If you're a principal who wants to be actively involved with staff selection — which is something that I recommend, at least to some extent — then one of the most important things you can do is provide (verbally or in writing) your manager, assistant, or agent with a very clear description of what you're looking for. A well-written job description will help your hiring manager successfully identify and select someone who can effectively do the job. (For information on writing good job descriptions, please see the previous chapter.) By painting a clear picture of what you're looking for, your hiring manager will be able to modify their thinking to meet your needs and preferences.

If you're an estate manager, house manager, personal assistant, HR professional, or other representative, then it is critical for you to gain a clear picture of what the principal wants. Effective communication about your principal's needs and preferences will make your job much easier and will help you find a great person for your employer. When possible, it's ideal to get a job description from the principal via email.

With a job description in place, you can now begin the process of finding candidates. Below are five methods for attracting applicants for the position at hand:

1) Running Newspaper Ads

Although newspaper ads may seem a bit outdated, I've found that candidates still read the help-wanted ads in their local papers. Moreover, the way that you word the ad for your position (whether it's an online ad or a print ad) has a great impact on the number and quality of candidates who respond. So, I encourage you to spend some time crafting your ad. Remember, your goal is to obtain responses from applicants who are well-qualified for the position you are looking to fill.

To achieve your objective, you should supply not only the essentials — the duties and responsibilities, salary and benefits (if applicable), location, living arrangements, etc. — but also a sales element. The late advertising legend David Ogilvy said it best when it comes to ads, and this applies to recruitment ads quite well: "Advertising is ... a medium for information, a message for a single purpose: to sell."

As an example, if you're located in The Hamptons and are

looking for a housekeeper for your residence, you would want to advertise in those publications to best target the candidates in your area. Running help-wanted ads in newspapers such as *The Southampton Press*, *Dan's Papers*, and *The East Hampton Star* would be a great place to start.

Below are three sample print ads that would likely attract strong applicants (note that given the costs of print advertising, these ads are shorter than online versions). Notice that the ads have a personal touch (referring to "We'd" and "You'll"), and they sell the positions by referencing a "great opportunity":

> Formal NYC household has a great opportunity for an experienced, personable Estate Manager. We'd prefer someone with at least five years of experience. You'll receive a competitive salary plus benefits. Email your resume to _____@gmail.com.
>
> Family of five in Boston has a great live-in opportunity for a caring, responsible Nanny for its three children. We'd prefer someone with at least three years of experience. You'll receive a competitive salary and benefits. Email your resume to _____@yahoo.com.
>
> Couple in The Hamptons has an exciting opportunity for a high-energy Personal Assistant. We'd prefer someone with at least three years of experience. You'll receive a competitive salary and benefits. Email your resume to _____@gmail.com.

2) Posting Jobs Online

While there is a wide range of websites that you may want to consider for posting positions online, some of the most popular ones include the following:

Indeed.com – Launched in 2004, this is currently the highest-traffic jobs website in the United States. For employers, Indeed uses a pay-per-performance pricing model, which means you pay for clicks to your job postings. For example, to start, you might run an ad with a cost-per-click of $1.00 and a budget of $100. Once 100 people have clicked on your ad, it will stop running (unless you increase your ad budget). You can search resumes for free, but a monthly or annual paid subscription is required to contact candidates. Indeed attracts workers in all types of fields, including household staffing. The company has headquarters in Austin, TX and Stamford, CT.

Monster.com – Created in 1999 and headquartered in Weston, Massachusetts, Monster.com is one of today's leading employment websites. It is consistently ranked among the top five employment websites in the United States. At the time of this writing, you can post a single job in one location for a 30-day period for $375. Discounted pricing is available for longer posting periods and multiple ads.

Care.com – Headquartered in Waltham, Massachusetts, this company helps families find childcare, senior care, special-needs care, tutoring, pet care, housekeeping, etc. On the site, you can search, post jobs, and view profiles of caregivers for free. To contact candidates and obtain background checks, you need to pay a monthly, quarterly, or yearly subscription fee.

While there are many other online media you can work with, including Facebook and the online versions of your local newspapers, the above websites offer a good starting point. For sample wording that you can model off of to create your own online ads, please see the job descriptions in the previous chapter. Since most online media allow you to write much more than you can in printed newspapers, you can use your full job description to make your Internet ads; many good, interested candidates will actually read the longer description.

Before closing this section, I would like to forewarn you that online recruitment sources can be very hit and miss. While recruitment always involves the screening of candidates, online job websites seem to yield a particularly high number of applicants who apply for positions for which they are simply not qualified. So, while online job websites offer one good way to recruit candidates, be prepared to spend some extra time evaluating applicants.

> WHILE RECRUITMENT ALWAYS INVOLVES THE SCREENING OF CANDIDATES, ONLINE JOB WEBSITES SEEM TO YIELD A PARTICULARLY HIGH NUMBER OF APPLICANTS WHO APPLY FOR POSITIONS FOR WHICH THEY ARE SIMPLY NOT QUALIFIED.

3) Obtaining Referrals From Your Staff Members

A simple and cost-effective way to identify potential candidates is to ask your current staff members if they know of any qualified people who might be a good fit for the position you're looking to fill. Oftentimes, individuals in the private service field, particularly those who have been working for some time, know of other people seeking work. You might even want to consider offering a bonus or thank-you gift for any staff member who introduces you to someone who you hire.

4) Obtaining Referrals From Your Friends and Associates

For a number of reasons other than job-related factors, domestic employees often discontinue working for their employers. It's common for a worker to leave their employer on good terms for some personal reason (e.g., an ailing parent or divorce), and later return to the domestic field. Of course, a household employee who leaves their employer is often replaced so that the employer's needs remain met. But good workers sometimes stay in contact with their past employers. When the former staff member is ready to re-enter the workforce, they may put the word out to previous employers. So, your friends and associates may know of well-qualified candidates already vetted (at least to some extent), who might be a great fit for your residence.

In addition, a household employee of a friend or associate may have friends or family seeking domestic work, and their employer may be aware of this. In such cases, your circle of friends can be an excellent source of candidates.

5) Working with a Household Staffing Agency

A good domestic agency can save you time and energy by pre-screening candidates for you and by providing a short-list of well-qualified individuals for your consideration. Seasoned domestic staffing specialists have seen thousands of resumes and interviewed a similar number of applicants. Accordingly, these specialists can bring to the table a wealth of knowledge and experience to help you find

> A GOOD DOMESTIC AGENCY CAN SAVE YOU TIME AND ENERGY BY PRE-SCREENING CANDIDATES FOR YOU AND BY PROVIDING A SHORT-LIST OF WELL-QUALIFIED INDIVIDUALS FOR YOUR CONSIDERATION.

the right person for your unique needs and preferences.

If you decide to work with a household staffing agency, it is essential that you perform due diligence to make sure the company is highly qualified. You'll also want to make sure you understand the firm's pricing and other requirements before you start receiving applicant information.

In assessing an agency, I recommend looking into the following:

- ◆ Google reviews
- ◆ Facebook reviews

- Awards and other recognitions
- Client testimonials
- Years in business
- Better Business Bureau membership and rating
- Licenses held (Does the agency hold the appropriate licenses to operate?)
- Fees and policies (A written agreement should be provided)
- Background checks (Are they done for all candidates prior to placement?)

Regarding its fee arrangement, the staffing agency should provide a straightforward written agreement so that all fees (and any other charges) are clear to you from the beginning. This is critical to helping prevent "he said, she said" situations from arising. By vetting the staffing company and having a clear picture of their fees upfront, you'll maximize your chances of having a successful relationship for hiring the right domestic employees.

It's also important to mention that, to my knowledge, all the major household staffing agencies offer some sort of trial period during which you can see how an employee performs before payment to the agency is due. It would be unusual for any staffing firm not to offer you the chance to see how a candidate performs before requiring payment for the placement. Some firms also offer a warranty period during which a replacement candidate is provided if the placed employee leaves or is let go from the position.

PART II.

HOW TO HIRE GREAT DOMESTIC EMPLOYEES

5. PROVEN TIPS FOR REVIEWING AND EVALUATING RESUMES

Resumes are usually the key written piece of information available to you to evaluate each job applicant, and it can sometimes be easy to lose sight of what exactly you're looking for. Harvard Business Review's *Hiring an Employee* notes that the three key things to remember as you're screening applicant resumes are:

1) A candidate's past job performance is a strong predictor of their future job performance. Psychologists generally agree that past behavior is a good basis for forecasting future behavior.

2) Together, the right experience; the right skills and abilities; the right personal characteristics (e.g., positivity and accountability); and the right overall fit for your household's culture make for a good match.

3) Be on your guard against aiming to hire somebody just like you, i.e., what psychologists call the "similar-to-me" bias. Instead, seek to find someone who is right for the particular position you need to fill (this point is relevant for managerial level and administrative domestic roles).

CHALLENGES IN EVALUATING RESUMES TO GET TO THE TRUTH

The challenge when screening resumes is that they often don't provide accurate representations of potential employees; rather, resumes can be viewed as job-seeker marketing pieces. In addition, it can feel tedious to read through stacks

THE CHALLENGE WHEN SCREENING RESUMES IS THAT THEY OFTEN DON'T PROVIDE ACCURATE REPRESENTATIONS OF POTENTIAL EMPLOYEES.

of resumes. As you read a resume, try to look past the surface information to get closer to what's really going on. The unfortunate reality is that resumes often contain inaccurate information and/or leave out information that would be helpful for you to know (and that does not reflect favorably upon the applicant).

In a 2015 survey by the employment website CareerBuilder of more than 2,500 hiring managers, the survey's authors found that 56% of hiring managers have caught lies on applicant resumes. It seems that the most common lie is the embellishment of skills or abilities. Upwards of 62% of the survey participants indicated that they came across such embellishment. Moreover, 54% of the hiring managers surveyed said that they found candidates misrepresenting the scope of their prior work responsibilities. About one-quarter of the hiring managers even came across applicants who indicated that they worked for employers for whom the applicants never actually worked.

A 2017 piece by Udemy, an online learning platform, entitled "This Is How Many People Are Lying on Their Resumes" also helps to show the extent of inaccuracy of applicant resumes. Udemy surveyed one thousand workers, and 26% of those surveyed under 40 years of age admitted that they've lied on their resumes. It is interesting to note that the incidence of reported lying dropped off substantially for individuals over 40 years of age: only 7% of people above 40 indicated that they've lied on their resumes.

> IT IS GENERALLY UNWISE TO ACCEPT INFORMATION PRESENTED ON RESUMES AT FACE VALUE.

Regardless of the exact statistics (there are many surveys out there, and they all vary a bit from one another), one thing seems clear: it is generally unwise to accept information presented on resumes at face value.

USING RED FLAGS TO AVOID HIRING ERRORS

You can gain a clearer picture of candidates by being aware of potential red flags as you evaluate applicant resumes. Here's a list of common red flags that I recommend looking out for as you evaluate candidate resumes:

◆ Jumping from job to job (i.e., a pattern of short-term employment)

◆ Gaps in work history

◆ Lack of a logical work progression (i.e., a pattern of flitting about in different fields)

◆ Excessive self-promotion (i.e., "I'm a visionary house manager")

◆ Poor overall resume structure and presentation (most relevant for managerial and assistant positions)

◆ Overly specific resume file names (i.e., "John Smith Houseman Resume" vs. "John Smith Resume" — in this case, John Smith may have experience that's all over the place).

HAVE TWO DIFFERENT STAFF MEMBERS REVIEW RESUMES

For household employers who rely on hiring staff to select their household employees, I highly recommend, when possible, having two different staff members review applicant resumes. While most principals' agents do a great job of hiring domestic employees, I have noticed that sometimes a hiring manger will automatically disqualify "overqualified" candidates. This can result in the loss of great people. When two sets of eyes review resumes, there's a good chance that at least one of the reviewers will want to interview an applicant who, at first glance, appears too qualified for the position at hand. Such seemingly overqualified candidates sometimes turn out to be among the best-performing employees at a residence.

In summary, as you read through resumes, remain open-minded yet skeptical, and keep in mind your overall goal: to find someone who will match well with your unique needs and preferences. Again, the combination of the right experience,

FOR HOUSEHOLD EMPLOYERS WHO RELY ON HIRING STAFF TO SELECT THEIR HOUSEHOLD EMPLOYEES, I HIGHLY RECOMMEND, WHEN POSSIBLE, HAVING TWO DIFFERENT STAFF MEMBERS REVIEW APPLICANT RESUMES.

the right skills and abilities, the right personal characteristics, and the right overall fit for your household's culture will make for a good match. Moreover, by 1) keeping in mind that many resumes are not accurate and 2) watching out for red flags, you'll greatly increase your chances of avoiding a problematic hire and increase your chances of finding someone who will excel in the position at hand.

6. HOW TO CONDUCT EFFECTIVE INTERVIEWS

The best way to conduct an interview that helps you effectively evaluate a candidate is to go into the interview with a plan and then execute that plan. It is a mistake to just "wing it" and rely on gut feelings. As Robert Half noted in his book, *Robert Half on Hiring*, your interviewing goal is not simply for you and the applicant to get to know one another. Rather, your goal is to determine whether the candidate may be a good fit for your position.

The two primary interview objectives are:

1) to gain valuable information about each candidate's personality, intelligence, background, skills, and abilities to determine whether they would be able to work effectively in the job, and

2) to communicate to applicants your expectations for the position at hand so that they can determine whether they believe the position would be a good fit for them.

To accomplish your goals, you'll need to assess each applicant's work history, skills and abilities, knowledge, and personality relative to the position at hand.

Psychologists generally agree that personality is among the best predictors of job success. According to an article entitled "Which traits predict job performance?" from the American Psychological Association (**apa.org**), while smarts are important, personality is key. Many of the most important drivers of job performance — including creativity, resourcefulness, leadership, integrity, attendance, and cooperation — are related to personality, not intelligence. Accordingly, you'll want to try to get a sense for what type of person an applicant really is. Ask yourself how agreeable, responsible, resourceful, and emotionally stable each candidate is. It's essential to determine if that person has the right personality for the job, not just the background, skills, abilities, and smarts to do the job.

You'll also want to pay special attention to whether an applicant has a true service orientation, as opposed to just the desire to collect a paycheck. Providing superior service is, of course, at the heart of domestic work. When a person has a natural drive to be of service to others, this bodes well for that individual's employer as well as for other staff members.

Empathy underlies a service orientation. As Adele Lynn, author of *The EQ Interview: Finding Employees with Emotional Intelligence*, points out, "When service orientation is born out of empathy rather than job duty, you have found the kind of employee who naturally wants to be helpful." While it is relatively easy to teach someone how to be helpful, it is much harder to teach a person to actually want to be of service to others. In the list of behavioral interview questions detailed below, I've included questions that will help you determine whether a candidate is naturally service-oriented.

> PROVIDING SUPERIOR SERVICE IS, OF COURSE, AT THE HEART OF DOMESTIC WORK. WHEN A PERSON HAS A NATURAL DRIVE TO BE OF SERVICE TO OTHERS, THIS BODES WELL FOR THAT INDIVIDUAL'S EMPLOYER AS WELL AS FOR OTHER STAFF MEMBERS.

With the above points in mind, it's also important to be aware of the reality of how applicants present themselves. A 2013 Harvard Business Review online article entitled the "Vast Majority of Applicants Lie in Job Interviews" noted that in one study, 81% of people lied about themselves during job interviews; moreover, more extroverted people were more apt to tell untruths. On average, participants in the study told 2.19 lies during each 15-minute interview. So, while it's good to be positive and professional, it's also important to be on the alert for less-than-accurate presentations of the truth.

Regarding the appropriate location for your interview, the venue you choose will depend on several factors, such as the source you used to find the applicant (e.g., referral or advertisement) and your personal level of comfort when meeting candidates. It often makes sense to schedule the initial interview(s) outside of your home, at, for example, a coffee shop, club, or domestic agency's office (if you're working with a staffing firm).

For the interview, each candidate should bring with them their current resume and color copies of two different forms of photo identification. By presenting to you a current U.S. passport or a driver's license and green card, the applicant can prove to you that they can legally work in the United States. (Each applicant must be willing to sign an I-9 form, indicating that they can legally work in the U.S.)

At the start of the interview, you can help put the candidate at ease by asking general questions such as "How are you today?" or "How was your trip here?" Throughout the interview, you want the candidate to be the one doing most of the talking — perhaps 80% or more of the time — so that you can learn as much as possible about their fit for your open position. Listening carefully is critical to your developing an accurate picture of each candidate. I should also mention here that it is important to be cautious about your own first impression. One person's first impression of an applicant — good or bad — is usually not a good predictor of whether the applicant will succeed on the job.

> BY PRESENTING TO YOU A CURRENT U.S. PASSPORT OR A DRIVER'S LICENSE AND GREEN CARD, THE APPLICANT CAN PROVE TO YOU THAT THEY CAN LEGALLY WORK IN THE UNITED STATES.

Broadly speaking, beyond background questions focusing on a candidate's work experience and training, there are three main categories of interview questions: open-ended, behavioral, and situational. Effective interviewers generally rely on a combination of these different types of questions to most accurately assess applicants. Below is an overview of each question category.

OPEN-ENDED QUESTIONS

These questions are called open-ended because an interviewee cannot answer them with a simple yes, no, or other fixed response. Open-ended questions are phrased in such a way that a more elaborate response is required — such questions leave room for an enormous range of answers. Because open-ended questions require the candidate to divulge information on the fly, they offer an excellent means to learn information about the person that might otherwise be hard to come by.

BECAUSE OPEN-ENDED QUESTIONS REQUIRE THE CANDIDATE TO DIVULGE INFORMATION ON THE FLY, THEY OFFER AN EXCELLENT MEANS TO LEARN INFORMATION ABOUT THE PERSON THAT MIGHT OTHERWISE BE HARD TO COME BY.

Examples of open-ended questions that you might choose to ask include:

- ◆ Tell me about a typical day at your last job.
- ◆ What were the most challenging aspects of your last position, and how did you handle them?
- ◆ What aspects of your last job did you like the least?
- ◆ Tell me three things I should know about you.
- ◆ What are your feelings about working on weekends?
- ◆ What are your feelings about working long days during the summertime?
- ◆ Tell me about why you think we should hire you.

◆ What do you think sets you apart from other candidates applying for this position?

BEHAVIORAL QUESTIONS

Behavior-based questions seek to find out information about an applicant's past behavior, which can serve as a guide for their expected future behavior. As psychologists generally agree that past behavior is a reliable predictor of future behavior, employers can use behavioral questions to help gauge how successful an applicant would be in the position at hand.

> BEHAVIOR-BASED QUESTIONS SEEK TO FIND OUT INFORMATION ABOUT AN APPLICANT'S PAST BEHAVIOR, WHICH CAN SERVE AS A GUIDE FOR THEIR EXPECTED FUTURE BEHAVIOR.

Below are examples of behavioral questions. Note that the first three questions explicitly aim to determine the extent of an applicant's service orientation.

◆ Tell me about an instance when you helped another person without being asked to do so.

◆ Tell me about a situation in which you helped someone even though the assistance you offered was not part of your job description.

◆ Was there a time at work in one of your previous positions when it made you upset to have to help someone? Tell me about that situation.

◆ How do you handle difficult situations? Give me an example from one of your previous positions.

◆ Tell me about a time that you had too many things to get done during the day and how you handled that.

◆ Were you ever unsuccessful at a task given by a past employer? How did you handle the situation?

- Give me an example of how you prioritized your work in your last position.

- Tell me about a goal that you set in one of your past roles and how you went about achieving it.

- Describe a time when you worked with a difficult colleague. How did you deal with that individual?

- Tell me about a particularly difficult day at a previous place of employment. How did you handle the day's work?

- Tell me about a time that you helped guide other people on staff to achieve the team's goals.

SITUATIONAL QUESTIONS

When using a situational interview question, the interviewer asks a candidate to think about a set of circumstances — an example challenge that might occur in the future for the position at hand — and then describe how they would handle the given situation. One advantage of these types of questions is that the interviewer can ask the same question of all interviewees and then compare their responses. Situational questions also prove valuable when the applicant does not have certain direct experience in the position at hand, and the interviewer wants to assess how the applicant would handle the new territory.

> WHEN USING A SITUATIONAL INTERVIEW QUESTION, THE INTERVIEWER ASKS A CANDIDATE TO THINK ABOUT A SET OF CIRCUMSTANCES AND THEN DESCRIBE HOW THEY WOULD HANDLE THE GIVEN SITUATION.

Examples of situational questions include the following:

- What if you had to work some seven-day weeks during a busy period?
- What if one of our other staff members was absent and you had to help fill in for them?
- What if you needed to travel with the principal throughout the year?
- How would you handle a situation in which you had to work together with a coworker who you found to be difficult?
- How would you handle a day during which you found it difficult to complete everything on your to-do list?

When interviewing, it's also important to keep in mind those areas — based on U.S. federal and state laws — for which you must not ask questions or take great care in doing so. *Hiring and Keeping the Best People* from The Harvard Business Essentials lists the following questioning topics that could get you into trouble:

- Age or date of birth
- Religion
- Marital status
- Intention to have children
- Race
- Gender or sexual orientation
- National origin, ethnicity, and/or ancestry
- Citizenship
- Disability or handicap
- Education unrelated to the ability to do the job
- Arrests and conviction records (note that your background check will reveal any issues)
- Garnishment of wages

For additional information about legal issues related to the hiring and employment of household employees, please see **Appendix II**, The Legal Landscape of Household Staffing.

Especially during the initial interview(s), it's also useful to take notes. While some people feel uncomfortable taking notes, note-taking by an interviewer is a perfectly normal thing. You might even choose to mention to the applicant at the start of the interview, "I'll be taking some notes to help me accurately remember what we discuss today."

Moreover, throughout the interviewing process, the safest way to go is the ethical way. Be straightforward and honest about the position you're looking to fill. Mention the negatives (or potential negatives) as well as the positives of the position to ensure that everyone is on the same page regarding the realities of the job. For example, if the position involves six- or seven-day workweeks during the summer, and not five-day workweeks, be upfront about that reality.

Bad things often happen when applicants get into a job and undesirable surprises arise. You want a candidate to be clear about what the job is and involves, and you want them to have no meaningful reservations about taking the job. In fact, I've found that when residential employee/

> YOU WANT A CANDIDATE TO BE CLEAR ABOUT WHAT THE JOB IS AND INVOLVES, AND YOU WANT THEM TO HAVE NO MEANINGFUL RESERVATIONS ABOUT TAKING THE JOB.

employer matches fail, it's usually for one reason: the employer or employee (and sometimes both) had an insufficient or unclear view of the expectations of the other party and/or the nature of the job itself.

It's important to keep in mind that during the interview, evaluation goes both ways: while you're assessing what a candidate can bring to the table, a good candidate will be evaluating whether they are interested in pursuing the position. Remaining present and in control of your emotions during the interview is essential to garnering the information you need from candidates and presenting yourself in the best light. Regardless of what is said, by "keeping your cool" you will be able to collect useful information about an applicant, make a good impression, and successfully lead the interview to its appropriate end (even if the candidate is a definite "no").

To close the interview, you might want to mention to the applicant that the interview is coming to a close. Thank them for coming in to meet with you. Depending on your level of interest in the candidate, you can advise them of the next steps. For example, for a strong candidate, you could let them know that you think they might be a great fit and that you will proceed with checking references. You can advise the candidate that you will get in touch with them within a few days regarding a second interview (it's often a good practice to meet candidates two or more times before making your decision).

For a weak candidate, you might tell them that you are interviewing a number of other candidates and will be in touch with them once your interviewing process is finished. Of course, it's always best to call or email those individuals who you do not end up hiring to thank them again for coming in and to let them know that you chose a different candidate who was a better match for the position.

After the interview, it's helpful to organize and elaborate on your notes while they are fresh in your mind so that you can have a good summary record of the meeting. If you're doing back-to-back interviews with many candidates, then I suggest allocating about five minutes at the end of each interview for wrapping up your notes. After you've interviewed a dozen (or even a half-dozen) candidates, you'll be glad you have your notes.

Once you have completed the initial interview(s), it's highly valuable for you to show the applicant the house and grounds. By doing a walk-through of the property with the candidate, you can conduct a "show and tell," providing more detail about

DON'T RULE OUT A CANDIDATE WHO SEEMS "OVERQUALIFIED" WITHOUT GIVING THE PERSON PROPER CONSIDERATION.

the requirements of the position at hand. This will help give the applicant a much better idea of what's required of the job. (If you're working with an agency and looking to hire multiple household employees, I would recommend having the placement specialist with whom you're working see the property as well.)

Before closing this chapter, I'd like to offer one more helpful tip. Don't rule out a candidate who seems "overqualified" without giving the person proper consideration. Unless there are other reasons for eliminating someone from your candidate pool, doing so because the individual seems too qualified is generally not a good move. Well-qualified candidates often have a variety of reasons for applying for the position at hand (e.g., cultural fit and benefits), and you don't want to lose out on making a great hire due to fear that the person is overqualified for the position.

7. CHECKING REFERENCES IN SEARCH OF THE TRUTH

Obtaining and checking valid references (as opposed to references only from family, friends, or others of questionable objectivity) is the primary means you have to verify your impressions of a candidate and the information they provided on a resume and during the interview. The best references that a candidate can provide are references from previous bosses. Ideally, an applicant should provide you with at least two work references (assuming the candidate has worked long enough to have a history with two employers). Moreover, while personal references can be useful in addition to professional references, by themselves they are generally insufficient.

Although reference letters are great to have since they can provide valuable information right away and before an interview is even arranged, reference letters should be confirmed by phone calls. When making calls to check references, start by opening the call clearly. When the person on the other end of the line picks up, it's good to be friendly and upfront about the reason for your call. You might say something like this:

> "Hello, this is Mr. or Mrs. _____. The reason for my call is that _____ (applicant's name) has applied for a position with us, and they gave us your name as a reference. Do you have a few minutes now to speak with me about the applicant?"

If the reference cannot speak immediately, then arrange a different time to speak that's convenient for you both.

Once you move into the questioning stage, it's good to begin by trying to verify the factual information of a given job: title,

> ### REFERENCE LETTERS SHOULD BE CONFIRMED BY PHONE CALLS.

dates of employment, responsibilities, etc. Then, ask questions that will help you gain a clearer picture of the applicant's experience, skills, abilities, intelligence, personality, work ethic, etc. Good questions to ask might include the following:

◆ Tell me about the applicant's strengths.

◆ How would you compare the applicant's performance to that of other people who did the job?

◆ What are the applicant's weaknesses?

◆ How was the applicant's attendance at work?

◆ How was the applicant's punctuality?

◆ How seriously did the applicant take the job?

◆ Would you consider the applicant to be an upbeat person?

◆ How did the applicant work with other staff members?

◆ What did the applicant's employees think of the applicant? (This is relevant in a case where the applicant was a manager.)

And, lastly, three of the most important questions you can ask are:

◆ Why is the applicant no longer working for you?

◆ Would you recommend the applicant to a friend?

◆ Would you hire the applicant again if you could?

Keep in mind that you will probably only want to choose around a half-dozen of the above questions to ask. In asking certain questions, the discussion may end up going in unexpected but useful directions. And, while references generally provide positive information about candidates, by carefully listening and probing when necessary, you can gain key information to make your decision. Moreover, while it's helpful to sound natural on the call (and not scripted), by sticking to your list of predetermined questions, you'll be more likely to have a productive call.

Before finishing this chapter, I'd also like to say a few words about using emails to obtain references. While I believe that phone calls offer the best means to check references (besides in-person meetings, which are typically not an option), it is becoming more common to do email-based reference checks. When time is of the essence, I suggest first trying to reach each reference by phone. For those people whom you cannot reach, send them an email. In the email, you can explain why you are contacting them and you can either: 1) list your questions about the applicant in your email or 2) ask the reference when would be a convenient time for you to call them to discuss the applicant.

8. THE FORMAL BACKGROUND CHECK

After you have carefully reviewed a candidate's resume, thoughtfully interviewed them, and thoroughly checked their references, the evaluation process requires one additional step before an offer should be extended: having a formal background check done. Conducting background checks is an easy and cost-effective way to reduce avoidable risks. With the Internet, you can complete a background check for around $30 to $60 per candidate — money that's extremely well spent should you uncover anything.

> CONDUCTING BACKGROUND CHECKS IS AN EASY AND COST-EFFECTIVE WAY TO REDUCE AVOIDABLE RISKS.

Studies support the need for conducting formal background checks. For example, ADP's 2009 "Annual Screening Index," which was based on nearly 5.5 million individual background checks completed during 2008 for a wide range of organizations, revealed the following:

- ➤ 9% of background checks contained an adverse record (concerning criminal history, credit, and driving records).

- ➤ 46% of reference and credential verifications revealed a discrepancy between information provided by candidates and what the screening revealed on employment, education, and/or reference checks.

- ➤ 37% of driving record checks showed one or more violation(s) or conviction(s).

- ➤ Approximately 6% of the criminal record checks revealed a criminal record within the last seven years (out of 1.7 million checks performed).

Another more recent study, conducted by HireRight, a company that provides on-demand employment background checks, also demonstrates the importance of performing thorough due diligence on candidates. HireRight's 2018 Benchmark Report, which surveyed over six thousand HR professionals, found that 84% of employers found a lie or misrepresentation on a resume or job application, and this occurred at all levels of the employer organizations. Background checks are a must.

One company that offers background checks and employment screening for individual as well as organizational clients around the country is SentryLink (**www.sentrylink.com**). If you're conducting the check on an applicant as an individual (as opposed to someone from a business), then the reports you'll want to purchase are:

1) National Criminal Background Check (essential for you to do) – This report provides a "comprehensive criminal check showing felonies, misdemeanors, sex offenses, and more at the state and county level." The check also includes results from the Office of Foreign Assets Control (OFAC), the Office of Inspector General (OIG), and terrorist watch lists. The price for this check at the time of this writing is $19.95. You can find out more about the exact coverage provided by visiting **https://www.sentrylink.com/web/ourData.jsp**.

2) Social Security Number Trace and Validation (optional for you to do) – "This report confirms that a social security number is valid and checks if the number holder is listed on the government death index. It provides you with all names associated with this SSN and includes counties and states of residence for performing a more extensive background check. The state and year in which the number was issued is also given." The price for this check at the time of this writing is $7.

SentryLink also currently provides a "Driving Record Check" for $19.95. However, the company advises on its website that it is "only permitted to sell driving records to established, non-home-based businesses, with a clear business need for driving records." For larger estates or household employers who also have their own businesses, you might want to complete SentryLink's required paperwork in order to run driving record checks. Note that SentryLink will "verify your business and its needs" before granting you access for running driving records reports.

When running background checks, it's important to be aware of the legal requirements associated with such checks. On SentryLink's website, there's a user-friendly list of employer FAQs (see **https://www.sentrylink.com/web/resource.jsp**). One of the key questions on the page is, "What legal requirements do I need to be aware of?"

SentryLink advises the following:

> *"For the [background check] report, we require a first name, middle initial, and last name, along with date of birth. A social security number is highly recommended. You must also have a mailing address and e-mail address for your applicant, which we will use for legal purposes only.*
>
> *You must obtain a signed release form from the applicant before running the report and comply with the relevant provisions of the Fair Credit Reporting Act. You must review the Obligation of Users under the FCRA and abide by its requirements."*

SentryLink provides a free, handy release form entitled "Employee Background Check Release." As with all legal matters mentioned in this guide, it's advisable to consult with your attorney to make sure that any release form you use complies with the laws in your jurisdiction. Visit **https://www.sentrylink.com/web/resource.jsp** for a Word version of the release form and additional information.

As a disclosure, I'd like to mention that I have no relationship with SentryLink, and I am in no way compensated by them. There's a wide range of well-respected companies offering online pre-employment reports. I expect that if you choose to conduct background checks for applicants directly, you'll find that it's fairly easy to find a good provider to meet your needs. Note that domestic agencies typically work with background check providers geared toward companies as opposed to individual clients. If you work with a domestic agency, once you are close to making a hiring decision, you may even want to ask the agency for a copy of the background report for the applicant you're considering.

9. CHOOSING THE RIGHT CANDIDATE

As you near the end of your candidate evaluation process, all candidates on your final shortlist must, of course, have the core experience, skills, abilities, and level of intelligence required for the position at hand. Moreover, as previously covered, you'll want to give the greatest weight to those factors that research has shown to be most predictive of on-the-job success:

1) a positive attitude in which one feels satisfaction from work;

2) accountability/the belief that one has direct control over work-related outcomes;

3) past-related job success, or a track record of meeting objectives close to the ones you would like met; and

4) cultural fit, which centers on shared values with the household and authentic interest in the job at hand.

One helpful exercise that Robert Half recommended is to try to envision an applicant in the job. If you are able to picture the person doing their duties well and fitting in nicely with your household — even on a difficult day — then you may have found your person.

Using a structured list as you evaluate a candidate can help you stay focused on the factors that matter to successfully narrow down your candidate list. *Hiring an Employee* from Harvard Business Press offers a useful list of factors to consider when you evaluate candidates. I have modified the factors as needed for residential employment and have also included Super Elements not detailed in the original list:

IF YOU ARE ABLE TO PICTURE THE PERSON DOING THEIR DUTIES WELL AND FITTING IN NICELY, YOU MAY HAVE FOUND YOUR PERSON.

- Personal characteristics, such as positivity, friendliness, resourcefulness, conscientiousness, and accountability
- Education and/or training
- Essential performance factors (Can this person do the work required? Do they have a track record of success?)
- Compatibility with your household culture (e.g., formal or informal) and your management style (e.g., hands-on or "please spare me the details")
- Elimination factors (Is there anything in the applicant's profile that suggests they cannot do the job well?)
- Essential technical expertise, such as security system knowledge, auto-care skills, and handyman expertise
- Overall assessment (What's your "big-picture" view of the candidate, all things considered?)

I also recommend giving special consideration to how much an applicant wants a job. Oftentimes, candidates who are very motivated to work for you and are excited about the position end up working out very well after you hire them. They also tend to stay for a longer period.

Lastly, I advise against settling for someone who you are not convinced can do the job well. In general, even if you feel you must find someone quickly, it's usually much better to wait to hire an individual who you feel confident can do the job effectively.

CANDIDATES WHO ARE VERY MOTIVATED TO WORK FOR YOU AND ARE EXCITED ABOUT THE POSITION OFTEN END UP WORKING OUT VERY WELL AFTER YOU HIRE THEM.

10. MAKING THE JOB OFFER

After you have gone through the process of evaluating resumes, conducting interviews, checking references, and having a background check done, it's time to decide which strong candidate you would like to hire. To make your decision, I encourage you to use the following simple process detailed in Harvard Business Essentials' *Hiring and Keeping the Best People*.

First, identify the top two or three candidates who you believe would be able to most effectively meet the needs of the available position. Then, ask yourself this about each person: "Do we want this person to work for us?" It's important to keep in mind that your goal is not simply to hire the person with the strongest credentials — it's to hire the person who will do the job well and who will also fit in with your household's culture (of course, for managerial and administrative positions, make sure to avoid the trap of trying to hire someone just like you). By considering both ability to perform and personality/cultural fit, you'll greatly increase your chances of hiring someone who will be with you for years.

> BY CONSIDERING BOTH ABILITY TO PERFORM AND PERSONALITY/CULTURAL FIT, YOU'LL GREATLY INCREASE YOUR CHANCES OF HIRING SOMEONE WHO WILL BE WITH YOU FOR YEARS.

If you have reservations about a candidate, it's a good idea to ask them to meet with you again for an additional interview. In the interview, take the opportunity to address any issues outstanding in your mind. You might also want to ask for additional references to gain a broader and clearer picture of the applicant.

For any final candidate, doing some sort of trial is hands-down the best way to predict whether someone will do well in the job. Before extending a formal job offer, it's good to advise the applicant that there will be a trial period — one day to two weeks is common — to ensure that you both are happy with the match. Even with proper pre-employment screening (interviews, reference checks, and background checks), there is always the risk of a mismatch.

The trial period that you ultimately arrange will depend both on your availability and factors such as whether the applicant is currently employed and where they are located. For example, for candidates who are currently employed, a one- to three-day trial often makes sense. For candidates who will be relocating from out of state, it is essential to have a trial period of, perhaps, one week.

The reason that some sort of trial is so very important is simple: the most significant driver in predicting future job success is actual success in the job itself. While necessary and useful in the hiring process, resume evaluation, interviews, and reference checks can take you only so far in your evaluation of an applicant. Rather, having someone actually do the job and evaluating that person's performance provides you with the greatest chance of finding the right person who will stay with you for the long term.

Concerned about a potential Housekeeper's ability to perform very high-end cleaning? Have the candidate work at your residence for a day or two. Not sure whether the Chauffeur you're considering is the one for you? Ask them to drive you for a few days. Concerned whether a Chef can prepare the type of cuisine you want? Ask them to do one or more tastings for you. (Note that for all trials, it is standard practice to pay candidates for the time they work.)

HAVING SOMEONE ACTUALLY DO THE JOB AND EVALUATING THAT PERSON'S PERFORMANCE PROVIDES YOU WITH THE GREATEST CHANCE OF FINDING THE RIGHT PERSON.

If the trial goes well, then you are ready to make your job offer. It's generally best to do this by phone (although some employers choose to use text or email). In making the offer, you'll want to show excitement about your new employee joining the household. Moreover, you'll want to discuss the core details of the position, including the title, starting date, compensation, etc. Depending on your particular situation, you may also choose to ask that the applicant let you know by a certain date whether they would like to accept the offer.

For certain candidates, it's also important to "sell" your position a bit. For example, in closing your offer conversation, you could mention to the candidate that you believe that their skills, abilities, and personality will be a terrific match for your household and that you think they will be very happy in the position.

The next step after presenting your offer is to mail or email a formal welcome letter. The purpose of the letter is to detail the particulars of your job offer and to offer protection for the employee and for yourself. As with any arrangement, it's best for all parties involved to be crystal clear about what they are agreeing to. In the next chapter, I'll talk about "Using a Welcome Letter to Get Everyone on the Same Page."

There's one caveat I'd like to point out, and it relates to candidates who ask for greater compensation at the time that you extend an offer. Once you get to the point where you are ready to extend an offer to a candidate, compensation should have

> AS WITH ANY ARRANGEMENT, IT'S BEST FOR ALL PARTIES INVOLVED TO BE CRYSTAL CLEAR ABOUT WHAT THEY ARE AGREEING TO.

been clearly discussed. Presumably, during preceding conversations, the candidate and you came to some sort of verbal agreement about compensation. If the compensation package agreed upon is job-appropriate and market-competitive, then an applicant generally should not try to ask for more money when you offer them the job. Such a request is, many times, a red flag. If you do increase your offer and the candidate comes on board with you, their tenure may be for a shorter period than you would like.

TAX CONSIDERATIONS
FOR HIRING HOUSEHOLD EMPLOYEES

Domestic employers often have questions about tax considerations related to hiring household staff, and for good reason. It's wise to carefully follow federal and state requirements. If you are interested in reading an overview of tax considerations for domestic hiring, please see **Appendix** III, Federal Tax Requirements for Household Employers. Please note that because state laws vary considerably, the appendix is focused on federal law only. It is beyond the scope of this guide to provide information for individual states. Moreover, your personal accountant is, of course, the best person to provide you with final advice for making decisions related to your hiring arrangements.

11. USING A WELCOME LETTER TO GET EVERYONE ON THE SAME PAGE

As in other professional dealings, it's best to put the particulars of the domestic employment relationship in writing to prevent misunderstandings and to protect both the employee and yourself. I suggest requiring each new employee to sign a "welcome letter" that serves as an employment agreement but is less threatening. The letter might be anywhere from one to several pages long. You may also choose to ask your new employee to sign an additional agreement later (below, I briefly mention the importance of having a confidentiality agreement).

As we'll cover in **Appendix II**, The Legal Landscape of Household Staffing, every employer situation is unique and the best person to advise you on your particular situation is your personal attorney. Accordingly, I'll include the obligatory legal disclaimer: *the information in this chapter is just that — information to use at your own risk — and it does not constitute any sort of legal advice.*

THE WELCOME LETTER

In addition to a positive statement that congratulates and welcomes the new employee, your welcome letter might include information such as the following:

◆ Work location(s)

◆ Work schedule

◆ Salary, benefits, and other compensation (with payroll frequency)

◆ Paid time off

◆ Responsibilities and duties (as clear and detailed as possible)

◆ Housing particulars for live-in arrangements (if applicable)

- Grounds for termination
- Drug and alcohol policy
- Disclosure about monitoring systems (if applicable)
- Requirement to sign separate confidentiality agreement

CONFIDENTIALITY AGREEMENT

In today's environment of instant online communication with enormous reach, I cannot stress enough how important it is to require employees to sign a confidentiality (non-disclosure) agreement. As members of your household, domestic employees have unusual access to your private information. A written agreement is essential to protect your family members, guests, and associates, as well as yourself. You might also want to consider including non-disparagement wording in your agreement. Your personal attorney can guide you most appropriately.

> I CANNOT STRESS ENOUGH HOW IMPORTANT IT IS TO REQUIRE EMPLOYEES TO SIGN A CONFIDENTIALITY AGREEMENT.

12. SIX TIPS TO HELP YOUR NEW EMPLOYEE START WORK SUCCESSFULLY

Getting employees started off well is a key aspect of hiring someone who will stay with you for years. According to an article by Harvard Business Review, "Your New Hires Won't Succeed Unless You Onboard Them Properly," the first three to six months are the most critical for new employees, as this is when they are particularly susceptible to turnover.

In fact, one study found that, on average, organizations lose nearly one-fifth of their new employees during the first 90 days. It's therefore easy to see why onboarding programs that work are greatly needed. Such programs support both new employees and hiring managers through proper socialization and strong professional support.

The October 2016 issue of "Wharton at Work" (produced by the University of Pennsylvania's Wharton School) provides great guidance on new-employee onboarding in its piece, "Onboarding Best Practices: Create Maximum Value from External Hires." The article notes that a formal, detailed onboarding process is essential to helping a new employee get quickly acclimated to your organization (a household is, of course, its own type of organization) and excel at their job.

The Wharton piece lists six steps, which I have modified below for a residential employment setting:

1) Introduce Your New Staff Member

For a residence with multiple staff members, identify the key people in your household who will be working closely with the new employee, and meet with them before the employee starts to communicate what the new employee's role will be. You should also develop a meeting plan early on between the new employee and their subordinates, peers, and superiors.

2) Educate Your Employee About the Household Culture

Explicitly teach the new hire about your household culture — what is expected and what is deemed to be inappropriate. You want your new employee to have a good idea about the character of your household so that they can most effectively join the other staff members and do their job well. Talk frankly about things that are important to you (as the principal) and be upfront about any pet peeves that you, other principals, or your house manager may have.

> YOU WANT YOUR NEW EMPLOYEE TO HAVE A GOOD IDEA ABOUT THE CHARACTER OF YOUR HOUSEHOLD SO THAT THEY CAN MOST EFFECTIVELY JOIN THE OTHER STAFF MEMBERS AND DO THEIR JOB WELL.

3) Prioritize Projects to Encourage Relationship Development

For a residence with a large staff, to the extent possible, prioritize projects that require your new hire to reach out to others working at the household, as this will help the individual form working relationships with key people faster. Keep in mind that the main challenge new hires face is a lack of relationships with people throughout the household. By creating good visibility for your new employee throughout the household, that person will have more opportunities to meet new people and to more quickly build relationships with them.

4) Assign a Mentor

For a residence with many staff members, assign a seasoned team member to provide support and coaching, and to help the new employee build relationships with others in the household. If there is a wide range of diverse skills that the new employee will be required to learn, it may even make sense to have more than one mentor for your new employee.

5) Check in With the Team

Check in after one, two, and three months with the new employee and with those with whom they work. The goal is to find out if the individual is effectively completing their duties and working well with others. Based on the information you collect, provide feedback to the employee (see Chapter 16 for guidance on how to effectively provide feedback).

6) Track Performance and Address Outstanding Issues

Monitor whether the new hire is acting on the feedback provided. It's detrimental to wait a month, or even a week, to resolve any matter that could be addressed in a timely manner. By addressing any concerns you may have right away, you can prevent small issues from becoming big ones.

PART III.

HOW TO KEEP GREAT DOMESTIC STAFF MEMBERS

13. THE IMPORTANCE OF KEEPING GREAT EMPLOYEES

While employee turnover is a natural, perfectly normal occurrence in even the most pleasant, well-run households, high turnover is costly to employers in a number of ways. There's the financial cost of recruiting new staff members — the salaries of the principal's hiring representative, advertising costs, agency placement fees, etc. There's also the work and aggravation associated with letting go of current workers and on-boarding new ones, and, for high-turnover households, there's the reputational damage that comes with being known as a "difficult" employer.

Unfortunately, I've noticed that in some households, turnover for certain positions occurs far too frequently — perhaps every six months to a year. This rapid turnover indicates that there is some sort of problem at the residence. For example, perhaps the position is far too demanding, or perhaps the existing staff are unwelcoming to new employees. House-

> HOUSEHOLD EMPLOYERS SHOULD BE AWARE THAT AVOIDABLE PROBLEMS LIKELY EXIST IF THEY HAVE A POSITION IN WHICH NEW EMPLOYEE AFTER NEW EMPLOYEE FAILS.

hold employers should be aware that avoidable problems likely exist if they have a position in which new employee after new employee fails. In such a situation, the principals of the house should spend some time investigating what is going on to: 1) ensure that the household culture is healthy, 2) ensure that the job requirements are not unreasonable, and 3) avoid unnecessarily paying agency or other recruitment fees again and again.

Below is an overview of the hard and soft costs associated with employee turnover.

1) HARD COSTS OF EMPLOYEE TURNOVER

Employee turnover is a problem that residential employers would do well to pay attention to. According to a 2006 study from the Center for Hospitality Research at Cornell University entitled "The Costs of Employee Turnover: When the Devil Is in the Details," there are five major cost categories involved with the total cost of replacing a staff member. These categories, which are detailed below and which I have modified for household employment, include pre-departure costs, recruitment costs, selection costs, orientation and training costs, and lost productivity costs.

Pre-Departure Costs

These costs are incurred after an employee has given notice that they will be leaving, but before they actually leave the job. Examples include time spent on dealing with change of health insurance forms, change-of-status processing, and severance packages.

Recruitment Costs

In order to fill the vacancy left by a departing employee, money and time must be spent on activities such as producing and distributing help-wanted advertising and enlisting the help of domestic staffing agencies.

Selection Costs

Selection of an individual from an applicant pool can be one of the most expensive components of the replacement process. There's interviewing, background and reference checking, and possibly travel expenses. If you work with an agency, this will represent perhaps your largest expense. Agencies generally charge a one-time fee of around 20% to 25% of each placed employee's first-year salary (for full-time, permanent placements), so the cost of paying an agency commission numerous times for the same position can be substantial.

Orientation and Training Costs

Even though new employees generally have the skills, abilities, and background required to succeed in their jobs, nearly every new employee requires at least some training, if only to understand a household's practices and culture. The main costs for orientation and training involve the time required by other staff members to provide training to the new employee.

Lost Productivity Costs

In a household environment, turnover hurts productivity in a number of ways. First, there's the decreased productivity of a soon-to-be-departing employee. Even in the case of good employees, short-timers are not likely to be as effective as those who will be continuing with the household. Second, all jobs have a learning curve, which can often take more time than expected. Third, there are disruption costs, as new employees often require training from other staff members or from their supervisor to get up to speed.

Of course, the higher level the job, the greater the turnover costs will be. For example, turnover costs will be substantially higher for an Estate Manager than for a Housekeeper.

2) SOFT COSTS OF EMPLOYEE TURNOVER

Besides the hard costs detailed above, it's also important to consider the soft costs of employee turnover, such as the following:

Potential Reputational Damage

"Difficult" employers typically become known among members of the domestic community, which is small. As a result, talented workers and the better domestic agencies may become wary of working with such employers.

Lower Morale Among Continuing Staff Members

In higher-turnover households, the loss of employees can lead to lower morale among employees who remain. Most employees value the good relationships that they have with their

> "DIFFICULT" EMPLOYERS TYPICALLY BECOME KNOWN AMONG MEMBERS OF THE DOMESTIC COMMUNITY, WHICH IS SMALL.

co-workers. Accordingly, the loss of valued colleagues can lower the spirits of the staff who remain.

Stress of Dealing With Employee Replacement

For principals and agents, a major cost of employee turnover is the stress of having to dealing with finding, evaluating, and hiring new staff members. Finding the right person for the position at hand can be a challenging and time-consuming process. Keeping great employees is an excellent way to help maintain your quality of life and peace of mind.

14. WHY PEOPLE LEAVE THEIR JOBS

In order to understand how to most effectively keep good employees, it's helpful to know the reasons why people leave their jobs. According to research revealed in Gallup's 2017 "State of the American Workplace" report, most employees quit for one or more of the following six reasons (the figures below indicate the percentage of workers who left their jobs for each reason):

1. Career advancement or promotional opportunities: 32%

2. Pay/benefits: 22%

3. Lack of fit to job: 20%

4. Management or the general work environment: 17%

5. Flexibility/scheduling: 8%

6. Job security: 2%

In considering the above percentages, it's interesting to note that employers have a great degree of control — perhaps north of 75% — over the reasons that employees decide to leave positions. Moreover, many of the reasons listed can be, at least to some extent, preemptively addressed by making sure that applicants understand the job, are fairly compensated at market-competitive levels, and fit well with the supervisor's management style and the overall household culture.

> FROM AN EMPLOYEE'S PERSPECTIVE, THE GENERAL WORK ENVIRONMENT, OPPORTUNITIES TO CONTRIBUTE, AND VALUES OF THE HOUSEHOLD ARE ALL HIGHLY IMPORTANT.

Glassdoor, one of the world's largest job and recruiting sites, did a similar study in 2017 entitled "Why Do Workers Quit?

The Factors That Predict Employee Turnover." This study involved over five thousand actual job changes from resumes in the company's database. The goal of the study was to evaluate predictive factors of whether an employee will stay or leave when they move on to a new role in a chosen career. A statistical analysis showed that three factors are most critical for employee retention:

1) organizational culture,

2) salary, and

3) degree to which the position was stagnant or offered some sort of growth opportunity.

It's clear that an organization's culture has a significant impact on whether an employee stays in their position, and that's why I stressed the great importance of thinking about your household's culture, values, and styles in relation to those of applicants when you evaluate them. From an employee's perspective, the general work environment, opportunities to contribute, and values of the household are all highly important.

It should come as no surprise that a higher base salary is another key factor impacting employee retention. We all have bills to pay and lives to live. Good domestic professionals are always in high demand. To keep your best employees, it's in your own best interests to make sure that they feel that their salaries are fair and market-competitive.

Lastly, opportunities to contribute more and take on additional duties are also valued highly by employees. Research shows that if an employee stagnates for a considerable time in their role, that person is significantly more likely to depart for a new position. Even in positions considered to be mundane, allowing some sort of variety and adding responsibilities are significant ways to help you keep good people.

15. WHY PEOPLE STAY AT THEIR JOBS

In the previous chapter, we covered the main reasons why people leave their jobs and, in doing so, we touched on the other side of the coin: why people stay. This chapter is closely related to the last one, but it focuses exclusively on what contemporary research tells us about the reasons why employees stay with their employers.

In 2012, the American Psychological Association (APA) — the largest scientific and professional organization of psychologists in the United States — released information on its Workforce Retention Survey, which evaluated the reasons that employees stay at their jobs. This detailed survey was conducted online by Harris Interactive, took place in August of 2012, and included responses from 1,240 employed (part-time or full-time) U.S. adults, aged 18 and older. Topping the list of reasons that employees stay were enjoying what they do and having work-life fit. Additional key information from the survey results is included in the following pages.

> BENEFITS SUCH AS HEALTH INSURANCE ARE CLEARLY HIGHLY IMPORTANT TO EMPLOYEES AND A MAJOR MOTIVATOR FOR EMPLOYEES TO REMAIN IN THEIR POSITIONS.

Of the Workforce Retention Survey participants, 60% cited benefits as a reason that they stay with their employer, while nearly the same amount (59%) indicated staying due to pay. Benefits such as health insurance are clearly highly important to employees and a major motivator for employees to remain in their positions. About 67% of respondents indicated that they remain in their current positions because they enjoy their work, and 39% of employees cited a lack of other job opportunities as one of the reasons that they remain in their current positions.

In an APA press release from August 28, 2012, David W. Ballard, head of the APA's Psychologically Healthy Workplace Program, was quoted as follows: "Americans spend a majority of their waking hours at work and, as such, they want to have harmony between their

> IT'S IMPORTANT TO KEEP IN MIND THE FACTORS THAT TODAY'S WORKERS VALUE MOST, AND TO TRY TO ADDRESS THOSE WORKPLACE ELEMENTS.

job demands and the other parts of their lives ..." Ballard also noted that, "To engage the workforce and remain competitive, it's no longer sufficient to focus solely on benefits. Today, top employers create an environment where employees feel connected to the organization and have a positive work experience that's part of a rich, fulfilling life." While domestic positions frequently have highly demanding schedules, to attract the best employees, it's important to keep in mind the factors that today's workers value most, and to try — to the extent possible — to address the workplace elements that employees value.

The Workforce Retention Survey also found that gender and age differences come into play. Below is a summary of key differences that were identified:

GENDER DIFFERENCES

➤ 72% of women and 64% of men cited work-life fit and enjoying their jobs as reasons that they remain with their current employers.

➤ Regarding workplace relationships, women more frequently cited co-workers as a reason to stay with their employers that did men (55% for women and 48% for men). Moreover, women were more likely than men to cite their managers (46% vs. 34%) and their connection to the organization (59% vs. 53%) as reasons that they chose to stay in their current positions.

➤ For benefits, pay, and the opportunity to make a difference at work, smaller gender differences were found to exist. For benefits, the figures were 61% for women vs. 59% for men; for pay, the figures were 57% for women vs. 62% for men; and for their job providing the chance to make a difference, the figures were 49% for women vs. 52% for men.

AGE DIFFERENCES

➤ Employees aged 55 and above were most likely to indicate enjoying their work (80%), work-life fit (76%), benefits (66%), a connected feeling with the organization (63%), and being able to make a difference (57%) as reasons that they stay in their current roles.

➤ Survey respondents in the 18-to-34 age group were, relative to other groups, least likely to indicate that enjoying their work (58%), work-life fit (61%), and benefits (54%) were the factors keeping them in their positions; these respondents were most likely to indicate that co-workers (57%) and managers (46%) are reasons to stay.

➤ 67% of employees in the 35-to-44 age group indicated that pay is a reason for staying with their employer, the highest of all the age groups in the study.

The survey also found that for employees who indicated that they planned to remain in their current position for at least two years, the main drivers of expected tenure included work enjoyment, having good work-life fit for the job, and having a feeling of connection to the employer organization.

A 2016 report by the Society for Human Resource Management entitled "SHRM's 2016 Employee Job Satisfaction and Engagement: The Doors of Opportunity Are Open Research Report" sheds additional light on the primary reasons that employees stay in their current positions. According to the SHRM report, employees identified the following five factors as contributing the most to their job satisfaction:

- Respectful treatment of all employees at all levels
- Compensation/pay
- Trust between employees and senior management
- Job security
- Opportunities to use their skills and abilities at work

Taking the above information in total, it seems safe to conclude that 1) striving to have a positive household culture, 2) effectively managing staff members, 3) offering competitive compensation and benefits, and 4) providing opportunities for employees to use their skills and abilities to productively contribute to the household will all help you keep good employees for the long term.

16. THE GIFT OF FEEDBACK

For many people who oversee others, providing feedback can seem like a time-consuming and uncomfortable act. Yet it is vital for you to give your employees feedback so that they can effectively do their jobs and you can have peace of mind. Michael Feiner, author of *The Feiner Points of Leadership*, says that "feedback is a gift," and I agree.

People strongly want and need feedback. Moreover, when leaders don't provide proper feedback, employees might end up assuming the worst. For example, without feedback, your staff members might think, "I'm not doing a good job" or "There must be a problem here." Even worse, an employee might assume "I don't really matter around here" or "I'm not important enough for my boss to give me feedback."

Sometimes employers are afraid to give feedback because they are concerned that it will deflate their staff members. However, withholding feedback only curtails employee growth and development. Feiner notes that feedback is a gift in two ways. It's a gift to the recipient because it provides data that can allow them to improve performance. And it's also a gift for the feedback giver. In providing feedback that helps employees improve their individual performance, a supervisor helps to ensure that the organization's overall performance improves.

In giving feedback, it's important to go beyond providing a simple "Good job," as this general statement, while encouraging, is not specific enough to guide an employee. Instead, explain to your employee what they need to do more of, less of, and differently in order to do the job better. Additionally, feedback should be provided on an ongoing basis, throughout the year, and in a timely manner if an incident requiring

EXPLAIN TO YOUR EMPLOYEE WHAT THEY NEED TO DO MORE OF, LESS OF, AND DIFFERENTLY IN ORDER TO DO THE JOB BETTER.

correction occurs. When you conduct your end-of-year performance review (which is valuable to do for each employee), put together a performance improvement plan for the upcoming year with your employee's help.

For feedback to work, it's critical that it be what Feiner calls "camera-lens": you should indicate the specifics of what you observed that led to your judgment of the employee's performance. For example, let's say that your Houseman did a poor job of greeting houseguests. It's not enough to simply say, "You did a bad job of greeting our guests today." That's just not helpful. Rather, you might say something like this: "When greeting our guests today, you seemed distracted and did not appear to be in a good mood. Also, you made the guests wait too long before you asked them whether they would like to get settled into their room." This sort of specific feedback will give employees a clear picture of their performance that allows them to adapt and improve in the future.

> FOR FEEDBACK TO WORK, IT'S CRITICAL THAT IT BE "CAMERA-LENS".

Giving Effective Feedback from Harvard Business Review Press offers excellent advice on the key factors that make for effective feedback. Here's what makes feedback work:

➤ It's shared frequently and in context — when a situation arises that requires your giving feedback, do so immediately and explain why you're addressing the issue.

➤ It aims to achieve a specific outcome — you must be clear on what you expect your employee to achieve so that they have a clear idea of what needs to be done to meet your requests.

➤ It is realistic in its expectations — no one is perfect; the feedback should focus on something realistically achievable.

➤ It shows respect for the recipient — in order to get buy-in for your feedback, you must present the feedback in a professional, straightforward way, without any tinge of irritation or of being judgmental; employees may pick up on subtle cues that show your underlying emotions.

➤ It is a two-way conversation — make your views clear to the feedback recipient, but also give them a chance to ask questions and make comments to understand your thoughts and to feel heard.

➤ It is expressed as a point of view rather than an absolute truth — by expressing your feedback as your reasoned opinion and not gospel, you'll make the feedback feel less judgmental and more constructive for the recipient.

➤ It assumes an opportunity for follow-up — you want feedback recipients to know that you will be monitoring their performance and will also let them know how they are doing as they move forward with their work.

Even when you provide clear, camera-lens feedback, some employees may not like hearing — at least initially — what you have to say. Feiner presents a simple model called the SARAH model, in which each letter of SARAH represents a phase that people often go through when they receive feedback that's perceived to be negative:

S stands for SHOCK. When first receiving feedback, employees are frequently taken aback by the information being delivered. They may even ask, "Where is this coming from? I've been working hard."

A stands for ANGER. It's common for feedback recipients to initially feel indignation, thinking something like, "I work hard around here. How can he say that!"

R stands for REJECTION. Some feel that your feedback is a rejection of their individual selves, and they may find it hard to get past this stage.

A stands for ACCEPTANCE. If the employee is encouraged to think about the feedback given (and the employee is sufficiently reasonable and self-aware), they will move past the first three stages and accept the feedback as having merit.

H stands for HELP. After having accepted the validity of the feedback provided, the employee can proceed to the final stage and seek additional help or guidance on how they can best act on the feedback to perform their job even better.

When providing feedback, it's also important for you to explain the consequences of your feedback. The employee should see how the feedback will affect their performance, the overall households' performance, and the employee's career and compensation (e.g., bonuses provided). Your employee should know "what's in it for me" when they act on your feedback.

Giving productive feedback is not easy, but it's worth the investment of your time and energy. As Feiner explains, "It takes time — a commodity that, for leaders in particular, is in very short supply — to give camera-lens feedback on an on-going basis. It takes guts for a leader to give negative feedback to a thin-skinned subordinate ... yet when leaders summon the commitment and the courage required, subordinates respond. Not simply because they know the leader cares about their performance, but because they have a clear picture of what they can do to improve it."

THE EMPLOYEE SHOULD SEE HOW THE FEEDBACK WILL AFFECT THEIR PERFORMANCE, THE OVERALL HOUSEHOLD'S PERFORMANCE, AND THE EMPLOYEE'S CAREER AND COMPENSATION.

17. RECOGNIZING AND REWARDING GOOD PERFORMANCE

As covered in previous chapters, employees in all different types of organizations consistently rate compensation among the top reasons that they stay at a job. And with inflation increasing yearly at a rate of around 2%, it's no wonder employees want some sort of raise even for doing the same job without providing better performance or taking on added responsibilities. With employees' cost of living increasing by about 2% annually, no salary increase means that their spending power actually decreases.

> WITH EMPLOYEES' COST OF LIVING INCREASING BY ABOUT 2% ANNUALLY, NO SALARY INCREASE MEANS THAT THEIR SPENDING POWER ACTUALLY DECREASES.

Savvy employers realize the value of providing cost-of-living raises. For example, I recently learned that one of my clients — who, although demanding, treats their domestic staff of around 20 people (across three residences) very well — provides an automatic 2.5% raise every year for all of their employees.

Glassdoor research reveals the importance of such annual salary increases: 35% of employees are so unsatisfied with their salary that they are willing to start looking for a new job because of it. And while an attractive household culture/environment helps keep people, it most effectively does so if employees are given market-appropriate compensation for their jobs. (See **Appendix I** for typical salary ranges for domestic positions.)

Small annual raises are the norm. For 2019, U.S. salary budgets are projected to rise by an average of 3.2%, up from an actual year-over-year increase of 3.1% for 2018, according to the WorldatWork 2018-2019 Salary Budget Survey. So, on average, employers are providing raises slightly above today's inflation rate. In the case of employees who perform well and/or take on additional duties, raises above the 3% level or bonuses equaling perhaps 5–10% of an employee's annual salary may be appropriate. It should be noted that these are broad figures intended to provide you with a general frame of reference. Your compensation decision will, of course, be based on your unique situation.

There are many other ways besides raises and bonus to reward your employees and keep them happy. A Gallup piece entitled "What Star Employees Want" highlights which attributes are most important to people when they are deciding whether to take a new job. Based on data collected from more than 31 million respondents, Gallup found that people most highly value a position and an organization that provides them with the following five things:

◆ The ability to do what they do best

◆ Greater work-life balance and better personal well-being

◆ Greater stability and job security

◆ A significant increase in income

◆ The opportunity to work for an organization with a great reputation

While Gallup's statistics come from a broad base of individuals in a wide range of organizations, from my experience, I believe that the five factors listed above apply well to household employees (although domestic employees are more used

IN THE CASE OF EMPLOYEES WHO PERFORM WELL AND/OR TAKE ON ADDITIONAL DUTIES, RAISES ABOVE THE 3% LEVEL OR BONUSES EQUALING PERHAPS 5–10% OF AN EMPLOYEE'S ANNUAL SALARY MAY BE APPROPRIATE.

to periods during which long hours and extended work weeks are necessary).

So, what are some perks and benefits that you can offer to your people? Here's a list of ideas for you to consider — of course, the individual ideas apply more to some domestic roles than others:

- A flexible schedule (days and hours)
- Reimbursement for commuting expenses
- Extra days off
- Gift certificates to local restaurants
- Gift cards
- Other gifts

There are also many ways to motivate your people that cost next to nothing, but that can be even more powerful than material offerings. Such motivators include a personal email to someone thanking

> THERE ARE ALSO MANY WAYS TO MOTIVATE YOUR PEOPLE THAT COST NEXT TO NOTHING, BUT THAT CAN BE EVEN MORE POWERFUL THAN MATERIAL OFFERINGS.

them for a job well done; an award or some other form of public recognition; and greeting cards on special occasions, such as birthdays, work anniversaries, and holidays.

This chapter includes just a small sampling of ideas for recognizing and rewarding good performance. There are countless other ways that you can reward and motivate your people. Only an understanding of what your people value and some creative thinking are required.

18. CLOSING THOUGHTS

Recruiting and hiring great people who will stay with you for the long term is rooted in using a sound process and keeping in mind the factors most predictive of on-the-job success. At the very start of your employee search, you'll want to think through the type of person who would do well in the position at hand and then develop a clear and accurate job description. The more clearly you envision the job and your ideal candidate, the greater your chance of hiring a great employee. It's also important to keep in mind potential legal landmines when recruiting and hiring (see **Appendix II** and speak with your attorney for more information) as well as federal and state bookkeeping and tax requirements (see **Appendix III** and speak with your tax professional).

Next, identify the recruitment practices that are best for you. Perhaps you want to search for candidates directly, or maybe you have decided that working with a domestic agency is the best way to go. Once you have strong applicants applying for the position at hand, follow all of the necessary steps to make an informed hiring decision: thoughtfully evaluate resumes; conduct structured, informative interviews; thoroughly check references from previous employers; and perform a background check to mitigate the risk of hiring someone who could turn out to be trouble.

Throughout your candidate-evaluation process, keep in mind that past behavior is predictive of future behavior and that smarts relevant to the job at hand are an important success driver. Also, look out for the four big Super Elements predictive of candidates' on-the-job success: 1) a positive attitude in which one feels satisfaction from work; 2) accountability/believing that one has direct control over work-related outcomes; 3) past related-job success, or a track record of meeting objectives close to the ones you would like met; and 4) cultural fit, which centers on shared values with the household and authentic interest in the job at hand.

Once you have carefully selected a great candidate and you're ready to make the job offer, call the person to let them know that you are excited they will be joining you, explain core starting details, and advise that you will be sending a formal offer letter. After your new employee has begun, use the six onboarding tips detailed in **Chapter 12** to start things off smoothly. Remember, most employee turnover occurs in the first three to six months, and proper onboarding fosters longevity of employee tenure.

To keep your star employees, address those factors most important to today's employees, such as a healthy household culture, market-competitive pay and benefits, opportunities to utilize skills, and the ability to contribute to the household's success. Also, be sure to provide timely, ongoing, and specific feedback so that each of your employees knows what they need to do more of, less of, and differently in order to do the job better. Remember, the costs for replacing an employee can be substantial, so reducing turnover for high-performing staff members is a worthwhile goal.

Lastly, great household professionals want to be properly rewarded and recognized for their hard work. By giving strong employees raises, bonuses, gifts, rewards, thank-you notes, and other motivators, you'll help ensure that you keep your best people for years to come.

APPENDIX I.

OVERVIEW OF DOMESTIC POSITIONS AND TYPICAL SALARY RANGES

Understandably, one of the first things that private service employers want to know — especially those who are newer to hiring domestic staff or who have not hired staff in some time — is how much they will need to pay their new employee. In this appendix, you'll find brief overviews of key domestic positions along with typical salary ranges. Keep in mind that the overviews are just that — brief and general position summaries — and that responsibilities and salaries can vary substantially from those provided. I've listed the domestic roles alphabetically for your convenience.

Butler

A Butler is usually responsible for a single residence. They maintain the household and supervise domestic staff to ensure all duties are fulfilled. At large residences, the house is sometimes divided into departments with the Butler in charge of the dining room, wine cellar, pantry, etc. A Butler is often a senior domestic staff member, and they may also provide chauffeur services.

In certain residences in which the Butler is the most senior domestic professional, titles such as Majordomo, Butler Administrator, Staff Manager, Chief of Staff, Staff Captain, and Head of Household Staff are sometimes given.

A Butler's responsibilities generally include ordering household supplies; setting and serving a formal table; caring for the silver, China, and crystal; greeting and seeing off family members and guests; and overseeing dinner parties, as well as other functions held in the residence. In addition, Butlers often have a good working knowledge of wines and can effectively use a computer.

Salary for a Butler depends on your location; the particular job requirements; the level of experience of the candidate; and benefits, perks, and other compensation. An approximate salary range for a typical Butler position is $65,000–$120,000+ per year.

Companion or Personal Care Aide

A Companion or Personal Care Aide, or Personal Care Assistant (PCA), helps those who are disabled or chronically ill with their daily living activities. Personal Care Aides assist clients with their personal, physical mobility, and therapeutic care needs. Typically, care is provided as per plans established by a doctor, rehabilitation health practitioner, social worker, or other health care professional.

In particular, a Companion or Personal Care Aide helps with

mobility-restricted activities, such as getting out of bed, bathing, dressing, and grooming. The Personal Care Assistant also may provide some basic health-related services, such as checking the patient's pulse rate, temperature, and respiration rate; helping with simple prescribed exercises; and reminding the employer to take their medication.

Personal Care Assistants may also be responsible for advising patients and their families on nutrition, cleanliness, and household tasks. Depending on employer needs, the Aide may change simple dressings, provide skin care, and more. A Companion may also accompany their employer to the doctor or on other errands, and the Aide may perform light housekeeping and homemaking duties.

A Companion or Personal Care Aide's salary depends on your location; the particular job requirements; the level of experience of the candidate; and benefits, perks, and other compensation. The approximate salary range for a typical Companion position is $52,000–$100,000+ per year.

Chauffeur

Upon request, a Chauffeur drives an employer, their family, guests, and others to social and professional appointments. They are also expected to care for the vehicle(s), making sure it is always clean and operating properly. A Private Driver may also be required to work in the office of the employer, filing or faxing and running errands. Hours typically vary, so a professional Chauffeur is generally quite flexible.

In most cases, proper physical presence is required by the Chauffeur at all times. This usually means that the Driver is neatly put together (i.e., conservatively dressed in a clean, pressed suit, dress shirt, and appropriately matching tie, with freshly polished matching footwear).

A Chauffeur's salary depends on your location; the particular job requirements; the level of experience of the candidate;

and benefits, perks, and other compensation. The approximate salary range for a typical Chauffeur position is $52,000–$120,000+ per year.

Chef

A Private Chef (or Personal Chef) is responsible for everything food- and kitchen-related at a residence. A Chef plans and prepares all meals for the employer's family and their guests (and possibly for the household staff), performs organization and kitchen cleanup, and shops for all food and food-related supplies.

A Personal Chef's responsibilities also include preparing food for parties, holiday meals, and special functions. These culinary professionals are generally highly skilled in preparing a range of dishes to meet specific taste and dietary requirements. A Private Chef can plan and prepare a menu ranging from traditional to gourmet, gluten-free, Kosher, vegetarian, or vegan, depending on preferences.

It is also common for a Private Chef to serve in a house-management capacity as well. In many residences, the Chef serves the role as both head of the kitchen and manager of the domestic staff. In such instances, Private Chefs are compensated at a higher rate for their additional responsibilities.

A Private Chef's salary depends on your location; the specific job requirements; the level of experience of the candidate; and benefits, perks, and other compensation. The typical salary range for a Chef is $80,000–$200,000+ per year.

Cook

A Cook is responsible for food preparation and kitchen/kitchen supplies management. They also help plan and prepare all meals for their employer family (and perhaps other domestic staff too, depending on the size of the household staff); organize and clean up the kitchen; and shop for all food and kitchen supplies.

A Cook's responsibilities also typically include food preparation for parties, holiday meals, and special functions. Household Cooks are generally skilled in making a variety of dishes to meet specific preferences. A Private Cook can also plan and prepare a menu ranging from family-style to cuisine-specific (e.g. Kosher, vegetarian, etc.), depending on employer needs.

Household Cooks often have multiple roles at a residence. For example, Housekeeper Cooks are typically responsible for cooking and the kitchen, and they also perform light housekeeping. Nanny Cooks perform cooking and kitchen management at a residence, and they also provide light nanny help for their employer family. Some Domestic Cooks are also required to drive, as needed. It is common for Domestic Cooks to be live-in or live-out staff members.

Salary for a Domestic Cook depends on the job location, the requirements, and the experience of the candidate. Benefits, perks, and other compensation also affect salary requirements. The typical yearly salary range for a Cook position is $52,000–$100,000.

Domestic Couple

A Domestic Couple is a full-charge household team, often a married husband-and-wife pair. The Domestic Couple typically has full responsibility for running the residence, and the position can involve a broad range of duties. Generally, these are live-in positions.

In a Domestic Couple team, one person is usually responsible for maintaining the inside of the residence: cleaning, shopping, menu planning, cooking, serving, doing the laundry, and overseeing other daily activities at the residence.

The other domestic professional is responsible for the outside grounds of the residence: gardening, light household maintenance, basic machinery maintenance, and vehicle care. In a situation in which an employer has a broader staff, the Domestic Couple may only oversee the inside of the house.

Additional Domestic Couple duties may include child care, event planning, expense reporting, elder care, and, in some cases, providing Personal Assistant-type support.

Salary for a Domestic Couple depends on your location; the particular job requirements; the level of experience of the candidates; and benefits, perks, and other compensation. The approximate salary range for a typical couple position is $110,000–$200,000+ per year (for both individuals together).

Estate Manager

An Estate Manager is primarily a chief administrator who bears broad responsibility for running an estate. This often involves overseeing and providing hands-on management for multiple residences. An Estate Manager's profile will vary depending on the individual candidate and the needs of the employer.

An Estate Manager assumes a leadership role among domestic staff members. They have a broad knowledge base relating to general household management duties. In addition, the Estate Manager will typically have a formal education, computer skills, and basic financial skills.

An Estate Manager's specific responsibilities, which depend on the size of the domestic staff, typically include hiring, directing, and terminating other household staff; liaising with and overseeing vendors and contractors; booking travel arrangements; maintaining household security; running errands; organizing and running large household events, parties, etc.; managing the household calendar; performing bookkeeping and other accounting tasks; and managing special projects.

Additional duties — particularly in a residence in which the Estate Manager works without others under their direction

— may involve Houseman or Housekeeper responsibilities. These duties include performing general handyman services and facilities/home maintenance tasks; maintaining household inventories; procuring supplies, including groceries; maintaining a proper indoor and outdoor appearance for the home; providing hands-on housekeeping (e.g., doing laundry and ironing; cleaning the kitchen, bath, and living areas; organization of closets, pantries, etc.; care for art, antiques, and fine furniture; etc.); driving family members to appointments and engagements; and more.

Overall, an Estate Manager endeavors to ensure that their Employer's life is as carefree as possible. They wear many hats and remain fully on top of all the details of the employer's residential life. The Estate Manager may live in or out of the residence, but the position is often a live-in role. Moreover, as needed, an Estate Manager travels with their employer's family, or alone, to additional residences and alternate destinations.

An Estate Manager's salary depends on your location; the specific job requirements; the level of experience of the candidate; and benefits, perks, and other compensation. The approximate annual salary range for Estate Managers is $100,000–$300,000+.

Groundskeeper

A Private Groundskeeper is a domestic professional who oversees landscaping, gardens, and other outdoor features to maintain an attractive appearance and proper functionality. To perform their job, a Groundskeeper must possess a wide range of knowledge of horticulture, pest control, and weed control. Moreover, Groundskeepers are skilled in the use of a wide range of equipment, such as lawn mowers, tractors, trimmers, edgers, leaf blowers, etc.

Although Groundskeepers often follow a site plan created by a landscape architect, many Groundskeepers are skilled in envisioning and executing new landscape design features, and they enjoy beautifying their employer's property.

A Groundskeeper's salary depends on your location; the particular job requirements; the level of experience of the candidate; and benefits, perks, and other compensation. The approximate salary range for a typical Groundskeeper position is $45,000–$100,000+ per year.

House Manager

A House Manager is typically responsible for overseeing and providing hands-on management of an Employer's residence. A House Manager may be the head domestic staff member to which other staff members report, or they may work under an Estate Manager. A Household Manager typically has a broad knowledge base, allowing them to effectively run a household.

Although a House Manager's specific responsibilities vary with the size of the household, duties typically include hiring, directing, and terminating other household staff; liaising with and overseeing vendors and contractors; booking travel arrangements; maintaining household security; running errands; organizing and running large household events, parties, etc.; managing the household calendar; performing basic financial management tasks; and managing and personally executing special projects.

Additional duties may include certain Houseman or Housekeeper responsibilities, such as providing basic handyman services and completing home maintenance tasks; maintaining household inventories; procuring supplies, including groceries, food service, and cleaning supplies; maintaining a neat and attractive outside and inside appearance of the residence; performing hands-on housekeeping activities (such as doing laundry and ironing; cleaning the kitchen, bath, and living areas; organizing closets, pantries, etc.; caring for art, antiques, and fine furniture; etc.); driving family members, associates, and guests to appointments and engagements; and more.

A House Manager's overall objective is to help make sure that their employer's life at their residence is as carefree as possible. Household Managers wear many hats, and they must stay fully on top of the many details of running the home. The Household Manager may live in or out of the residence, but the position is often a live-in role.

Salary for a House Manager depends on your location; the specific job requirements; the level of experience of the candidate; and benefits, perks, and other compensation. The approximate annual salary range for House Managers is $75,000–$200,000+.

Housekeeper

A Housekeeper is an individual responsible for the cleaning and maintenance of the interior of a residence. Typical domestic duties include cleaning, laundry, ironing, dusting, silver polishing, vacuuming, pet care, and running errands. Housekeeper duties may also include preparation of meals and caring for children. Housekeepers may be part-time or full-time, and live-in or live-out, depending on the employer's needs.

In larger residences, a Housekeeper (or Executive Housekeeper) may also be responsible for managing other Housekeepers and subordinate domestic staff members. In general, the staff of a large residence is divided into departments, and the Housekeeper oversees all of the cleaning staff, while the kitchen staff report to the Chef, and the between staff report to the Butler.

Salary for a Housekeeper depends on your location; the particular job requirements; the level of experience of the candidate; and benefits, perks, and other compensation. The salary range for a typical Housekeeper position is $52,000–$85,000 per year.

Housekeeper, Executive

An Executive Housekeeper (or Head Housekeeper) is responsible for managing Housekeepers and other subordinate domestic staff members. In general, the staff of a large residence is divided into departments, and the Executive Housekeeper oversees all the domestic workers performing housekeeping functions.

As the Executive Housekeeper is ultimately responsible for the work of the rest of the Housekeepers on staff, they manage the following activities: interior and exterior cleaning, laundering of clothes and linens, ironing, dusting, silver polishing, vacuuming, pet care, and supplies management. Head Housekeepers may be live-in or live-out, depending on the employer's needs. Moreover, they are generally hands-on in their daily work, guiding and working with other Housekeepers to simply get done what needs to be done.

Salary for an Executive Housekeeper depends on your location; the particular job requirements; the level of experience of the candidate; and benefits, perks, and other compensation. The typical salary range for an Executive Housekeeper position is $70,000–$100,000+ per year.

Houseman

A Houseman is generally tasked with the daily "hands-on" duties in a residence and is often counted on to help ensure the smooth and orderly running of the house. Responsibilities include heavy housework, such as cleaning floors, vacuuming, polishing silver, accepting heavy deliveries, and moving furniture and other items. A Houseman may also perform a range of other duties, such as filling in for the Housekeeper if they call in sick, watching the children, or helping the Chef in preparation for a formal dinner party.

The Houseman may also be required to care for the core grounds of a residence, including the main entry area of the house and the walkways. In a household in which there is only a Houseman (i.e., not additional domestic staff), the Houseman also typically does what a Housekeeper would be required to do and may have certain driving duties as well. In residences that have broader domestic staffs, The Houseman may also serve as a "right-hand man" to an Estate or Household Manager or to another domestic staff leader. Houseman may be live-in or live-out.

A Houseman's salary depends on your location; the particular job requirements; the level of experience of the candidate; and benefits, perks, and other compensation. The approximate annual salary range for Housemen is $52,000–$85,000+ per year.

Laundress

A Private Laundress is responsible for washing, ironing, and steaming their employers' clothes, bedding, dining linens, etc. The Laundress also puts away and organizes clothing, sheets, table linens, and other items in the household's closets and dressers. Additionally, they may be responsible for cleaning and polishing shoes, boots, etc.

Salary for a Laundress depends on your location; the particular job requirements; the level of experience of the candidate; and benefits, perks, and other compensation. The typical annual salary range for a Laundress is $52,000–$85,000.

Maid

Maids perform typical domestic chores, such as cooking, ironing, washing, cleaning the house, grocery shopping, vacuuming, pet care, taking care of children, and running errands. Some Maids are required to wear a uniform. Maids may be live-in or out, depending on the employer's needs.

In large households, Maids traditionally have a fixed position and specific role in the hierarchy of domestic staff. Moreover, while there is overlap among the various Maid positions (depending on the household's size) the positions themselves would generally be rigidly adhered to. A few of the key classifications of Maid roles in a large household include:

Lady's maid — reports directly to the Lady of the House and accompanies the Lady of the House on travel.

House Maid — performs visible functions and thus usually has a senior position; in a household in which there are multiple House Maids, they often fill more specialized positions, such as Chamber Maid or Laundry Maid.

Kitchen Maid — reports to the Chef and aids in running the kitchen.

Nursery Maid — works in the children's nursery (under the Nanny), maintaining a clean and orderly environment.

Salary for a Maid depends on your location; the particular job requirements; the level of experience of the candidate; and benefits, perks, and other compensation. The typical annual salary range for Maids is $52,000–$85,000.

Nanny

A Nanny (or Manny/Male Nanny) is a domestic professional who provides care for one or more children in an employer's family. Key responsibilities of a Nanny include organizing and coordinating the children's activities, preparing their meals, and keeping their rooms and play areas clean. Additional duties might include driving, doing the children's laundry, performing light cleaning, doing light cooking, running errands, providing tutoring, etc.

Nannies, like other domestic workers, may live in or out of their employer's residence, depending on their circumstances and those of their employer. Professional Nannies are often knowledgeable about first aid, and they have strong experience in childcare. Moreover, a Nanny, particularly one in more of a Governess role, may have attended college for several years or have a college degree.

A Nanny's salary depends on your location; the specific job requirements; the level of experience of the candidate; and benefits, perks, and other compensation. The annual typical salary range for Nannies is $52,000–$150,000+.

Personal Assistant

A Personal Assistant (also known as a PA, Family Assistant, Social Secretary, or Executive Assistant) is responsible for keeping up with the social and professional demands of their employer. Personality fit is particularly critical for the Personal Assistant position, as the role involves more of a one-on-one relationship with the employer than many other domestic positions.

A Personal Assistant's core responsibilities include keeping track of their employer's family agenda, arranging for reservations for various events, making travel arrangements, planning events, tending to the needs of guests, purchasing gifts and other items, performing certain secretarial duties, and running errands.

In some cases, a PA may serve as both an assistant and a house manager. In the house manager aspect of their role, these professionals manage (and hire and fire) other staff, oversee vendors, and assume other managerial-level duties. In such cases, PAs generally receive higher salaries to compensate them for the additional responsibilities.

A Personal Assistant's salary depends on your location; the particular job requirements; the level of experience of the candidate; and benefits, perks, and other compensation. The typical salary range for Personal Assistants is $65,000–$200,000+ per year.

Security Guard

A Private Security Guard (or Private Security Officer) is a professional who protects an individual employer and the employer's family. A Private Security Officer's primary duty is the prevention and deterrence of crime. Security officers are generally uniformed in a suit and tie (depending on the climate and season).

In particular, Private Security Guards act to protect their employers and the employers' property by 1) maintaining a high-visibility presence that deters illegal and inappropriate actions and 2) observing (either directly, through patrols, or by watching alarm systems or video cameras) for signs of crime, fire, or disorder, and then taking action and reporting any incidents to their employer and authorities (as needed).

Security Guards may also perform access control at building entrances and vehicle gates. That is, the Guards ensure that employees and visitors provide proper identification before entering an employer's premises. Private Security Officers are often called upon to respond to minor emergencies (lost persons, lockouts, dead vehicle batteries, etc.) and to assist in serious emergencies by guiding emergency responders to the scene of the incident, by helping to redirect foot traffic to safe locations, and by documenting what happened on an incident report. Moreover, Armed Security Officers are frequently contracted to respond as law enforcement until a given situation at a client location is under control and/or public authorities arrive on the scene.

A Security Guard's salary depends on your location; the specific job requirements; the level of experience of the candidate; and benefits, perks, and other compensation. The typical yearly salary range for Security Guards is $52,000–$125,000+.

Senior Care Aide

Senior Care Aides help the elderly with a wide range of medical and physical needs. Such Aides provide assistance on a temporary or full-time basis, depending on their employer's specific life situation. In addition to meeting home health needs, a Senior Aide may accompany the senior to the doctor or on other errands. The Aide may also perform light house-keeping and other home care duties such as basic maintenance and basic grounds care.

Home Health Aides (HHAs) or Personal Care Aides (PCAs) help seniors (and others) who are disabled, chronically ill, or cognitively impaired. Home Health Aides assist seniors with their personal, physical mobility, and therapeutic care needs. Generally, care is provided according to plans established by a doctor, rehabilitation health practitioner, social worker, or other health care professional.

In particular, an HHA helps the senior with mobility-restricted activities, such as getting out of bed, bathing, dressing, and grooming. The Home Health Aide also reminds a senior when to take their medication, and the Aide can check vital signs under the direction of a nurse or other healthcare practitioner. A Senior Care Aide may be responsible for advising the patient and the patient's family on nutrition, cleanliness, and household tasks. The Aide may also change simple dressings, provide skin care, and more.

Certified Nursing Assistants (CNAs) work under the guidance of a Registered Nurse (RN) or a Licensed Practical Nurse (LPN) to offer basic help to seniors and other patients. CNAs offer many of the services that Home Health Aides provide (see above) and more. A Certified Nursing Assistant stays in close company with their employer and looks after their grooming, bathing, and feeding.

Typical CNA job duties include serving meals, making beds, emptying bedpans, and helping patients to dress and bathe. In addition, CNAs assist nurses with necessary medical equipment, and they note down patient vitals and report them to nurses. As is the case with Home Health Aides, one of the Certified Nursing Assistant's most important roles is offering emotional support to the senior for whom they're caring.

Salary for a Senior Care Aide depends on your location; the specific job requirements; the level of experience of the candidate; and benefits, perks, and other compensation. The approximate annual salary range for Senior Aides is $52,000–$100,000+ per year.

Private Event Staffing

In addition to providing permanent and seasonal domestic staff, some agencies also provide private event staff to their clients. Even with staff in place, residential employers sometimes find that they need additional help with dinners, luncheons, parties, and other special events.

Event professionals that agencies typically provide include the following:

- Bartenders
- Bathroom Attendants
- Chefs and Sous Chefs
- Cleaning Staff
- General Helpers
- Greeters
- Grillers
- Kitchen Helpers
- Housemen
- Security Officers (armed or unarmed)
- Servers
- Staff Captains
- Other Staff

Event staff are normally paid an hourly rate or a day rate, depending on the position and the work venue. For example, in The Hamptons and New York City, Bartenders and Servers are typically billed at a rate of $40–$65 per hour. It is standard practice for households to tip event staff workers. For a five-hour event, a $50–$100 tip per worker is common.

APPENDIX II.

THE LEGAL LANDSCAPE OF HOUSEHOLD STAFFING

Having knowledge of federal and state laws related to domestic hiring and employment is essential to protecting yourself. As someone who is immersed in the private service field, I can tell you that more and more domestic workers are, rightly, becoming aware of the laws that govern their employment. Accordingly, it is more important than ever for household employers to "play by the rules" of employing domestic staff.

I also recommend that you stay abreast of changes in domestic employment law. In November of 2018, the first National Domestic Workers Bill of Rights was unveiled by the National Domestic Workers Alliance (NDWA), a labor advocacy group founded in 2007. The bill would affect pay levels and working conditions for domestic workers, and some expect that legislation will be introduced to Congress this year (2019). You can track developments related to the proposed bill at **www. domesticworkers.org**.

I expect that you'll find the information in this section helpful; however, I must emphasize that every employer situation is unique. Moreover, while my attorney, Steven T. Russell of Bayport, NY (see **http://www.bayportlaw.com**), was kind enough to review the material contained herein, the best person to advise you on your unique situation is your personal attorney. Accordingly, I'll include the obligatory legal disclaimer here: *the information in this book is just that — information that, if used, is done so at your own risk — and it does not constitute any sort of legal advice.*

With that said, let's dig into the legal landscape of domestic employment. The key regulators within the domestic employment industry are:

1) the U.S. Department of Labor,

2) the Equal Employment Opportunities Commission,

3) various departments and agencies within the individual state and many local governments,

4) the Internal Revenue Service, and

5) U.S. Citizenship and Immigration Services.

While the number and mix of legal requirements can be overwhelming, domestic employers who do not adhere to federal, state and local laws can expose themselves to fines and lawsuits. The following sections provide key information directly from the U.S. Department of Labor, the U.S. Equal Employment Opportunities Commission, and the other main regulators. The information below is current as of the time of this writing.

1) U.S. DEPARTMENT OF LABOR (DOL) REQUIREMENTS

A good place to start in reviewing the DOL's requirements is the "homecare" frequently asked questions page from the department's website, which is located here:

https://www.dol.gov/whd/homecare/faq.htm

This page provides an excellent overview of The Fair Labor Standards Act (FLSA), which is a body of federal law covering wages, as they relate to domestic workers (please note: while the above-referenced web page has "homecare" in its URL, the information applies to domestic service workers broadly). In 1938, Congress passed the FLSA "to provide minimum wage and overtime protections for workers, to prevent unfair competition among businesses based on subminimum wages, and to spread employment by requiring employers whose employees work excessive hours to compensate employees at one-and-one-half times the regular rate of pay for all hours worked over 40."

While the FLSA did not initially protect domestic workers, such as cooks, housekeepers, maids, and gardeners, Congress extended coverage to "domestic service" workers in 1974. The FLSA now applies to "employees performing household services in a private home, including those domestic service workers employed directly by households or by companies too small to be covered as enterprises under the Act."

Although the 1974 amendments of the FLSA extended coverage to domestic employees, certain workers remain exempt from the FLSA's minimum wage and overtime provisions. Specifically, "casual babysitters and domestic service workers employed to provide 'companionship services' to elderly persons or persons with illnesses, injuries, or disabilities are not required to be paid the minimum wage or overtime pay. Congress also created an exemption only from the overtime pay requirement for live-in domestic service workers." The Department of Labor issued final regulations in 1975 to implement these exemptions, and there has been little revision of domestic service wage regulations since that time.

Below is additional information about the provisions of the FLSA, including who the DOL defines as a domestic employer, who the DOL defines as a domestic worker, and what the DOL requires of households that employ domestic workers. For accuracy — and given the technical nature of the subject — much of the information is taken word-for-word from the DOL's website.

Question 1: What does it mean to be an employer under the Fair Labor Standards Act (which governs employers, including household employers)?

Answer: The Fair Labor Standards Act (FLSA) defines "employer" as any person acting directly or indirectly in the interest of an employer in relation to an employee. The FLSA further defines an "employee" as any individual employed by an employer and "employ" as to suffer or permit to work. The definition of employer is necessarily a broad one, in accordance with the remedial purpose of the FLSA.

> *"An individual, family, or household receiving services provided by a direct care worker typically acts as an 'employer' of the direct care worker under the FLSA. A single individual may be considered an employee of more than one employer under the FLSA. For example, an agency that sends a direct care worker to an individual's home may be a joint employer with the individual, family or household to whom the direct care worker provides services."*

For more information relating to the employment relationship, please see the following DOL Fact Sheet (#13):

https://www.dol.gov/whd/regs/compliance/whdfs13.pdf

This document provides general information concerning the meaning of "employment relationship" and the significance of that determination in applying provisions of the FLSA.

So, who exactly qualifies as a domestic worker? According to the DOL,

> "Domestic service workers provide services of a household nature in or about a private home. Persons employed in domestic service in private homes are covered by the FLSA. Domestic service workers include companions, babysitters, cooks, waiters, maids, housekeepers, nannies, nurses, janitors, caretakers, handymen, gardeners, home health aides, personal care aides, and family chauffeurs. Services that are not performed in or about a private home are not considered 'domestic service employment' under the FLSA."

Now that we've covered how the DOL defines the terms "household employer" and "household employee," we can turn to the DOL's employer requirements. DOL Fact Sheet #13: Employment Relationship Under the Fair Labor Standards Act (FLSA) explains that employers must abide by the following requirements:

> "When it has been determined that an employer-employee relationship does exist, and the employee is engaged in work that is subject to the Act, it is required that the employee be paid at least the Federal minimum wage of ... $7.25 per hour [($9.25 per hour if the household has four or more employees)] effective July 24, 2009, and in most cases overtime at time and one-half his/her regular rate of pay for all hours worked in excess of 40 per week."

Of course, for employers located in a state that has a minimum wage higher than the federal minimum wage, the employers must abide by the state requirements.

In addition to its wage rules, the FLSA also stipulates recordkeeping requirements. DOL Fact Sheet #79C: Recordkeeping Requirements for Individuals, Families, or Households Who Employ Domestic Service Workers Under the Fair Labor Standards Act (FLSA), provides information about employee records that must be maintained:

> "Employers subject to the FLSA must make, keep, and preserve records for each domestic service worker who is entitled to minimum wage and/or overtime pay. The law requires no particular form of records, but does require that the records include certain information about the employee and data about the hours worked and wages earned. (See 79F: Paid Family or Household Members in Certain Medicaid-Funded and Certain Other Publicly Funded Programs Offering Home Care Services Under the Fair Labor Standards Act (FLSA) for information on determining whether a domestic service worker employed by an individual, family or household must be paid minimum wage and overtime pay.) The employer may require a domestic service worker to record all hours worked and submit the record to the employer.
>
> The obligation to make and keep records, however, is the responsibility of the employer.
>
> Basic records that an employer must maintain include:
>
> (1) Employee's full name and social security number;
>
> (2) Home address, including zip code;
>
> (3) Hours worked each workday and total hours worked each workweek;
>
> (4) Total cash wages paid each week to the employee by the employer;
>
> (5) Weekly sums claimed by the employer for board, lodging or other facilities; and
>
> (6) Extra pay for weekly hours worked in excess of 40 by the employee for the employer."

2) EQUAL EMPLOYMENT OPPORTUNITIES COMMISSION (EEOC) REQUIREMENTS

Another U.S. organization that sets regulations for household employers is the Equal Employment Opportunity Commission (EEOC). The EEOC enforces Federal laws prohibiting employment discrimination. In this section, to ensure accuracy, much of the information is taken word-for-word (or with only very minor modifications) from the EEOC's website (please see **https://www.eeoc.gov/employers** for additional information).

EEOC laws protecting workers against employment discrimination cover the following:

➤ Unfair treatment because of a person's race, color, religion, sex (including pregnancy, gender identity, and sexual orientation), national origin, age (40 or older), disability or genetic information.

➤ Harassment by managers, co-workers, or others in a person's workplace, because of the individual's race, color, religion, sex (including pregnancy, gender identity, and sexual orientation), national origin, age (40 or older), disability, or genetic information.

➤ Denial of a reasonable workplace accommodation that a person needs because of their religious beliefs or disability.

➤ Retaliation because a person complained about job discrimination or assisted with a job discrimination investigation or lawsuit.

It is important to note that not all workers are covered by the EEOC's laws. The EEOC website explains,

"An employer must have a certain number of employees to be covered by the laws we enforce. This number varies depending on the type of employer (for example, whether the employer is a private company, a state or local government agency, a federal agency, an employment agency, or a labor

union) and the kind of discrimination alleged (for example, discrimination based on a person's race, color, religion, sex (including pregnancy, gender identity, and sexual orientation), national origin, age (40 or older), disability or genetic information)."

Below is more in-depth information from the EEOC's website about when the organization's laws apply:

General Coverage

If an employee has a complaint against a business (or some other private employer) that involves race, color, religion, sex (including pregnancy), national origin, age (40 or older), disability or genetic information, the business (or other organization) is subject to the EEOC regulation if it has 15 or more employees who worked for the employer for at least 20 calendar weeks (in this year or last).

Age Discrimination and Coverage

If an employee's complaint involves age discrimination, the business (or other organization) is subject to the laws the EEOC enforces if it has 20 or more employees who worked for the organization for at least 20 calendar weeks (in this year or last).

Equal Pay Act and Coverage

Virtually all employers are subject to the Equal Pay Act (EPA), which makes it illegal to pay different wages to men and women if they perform substantially equal work in the same workplace.

Deciding Coverage of Business/Private Employers

Figuring out whether you are covered by the EEOC's laws can be complicated. If you aren't sure about whether coverage exists, you should contact one of the EEOC field offices as soon as possible to get help with making that decision. It is also important to keep in mind that, even if an employer is not subject to regulation by the EEOC for employment discrimination, such employer will likely be regulated by state and local authorities for same. Both New York State and New York City, for example, have promulgated Human Rights laws that (among other things) prohibit unlawful discrimination by employers.

You can find the appropriate EEOC office to contact by using the lookup tool on the EEOC's website at **https://www.eeoc. gov/field.**

Lastly, it's important to point out that people not employed by an employer, such as independent contractors, aren't covered by the EEOC's anti-discrimination laws. Figuring out whether a person is an employee of an organization (as opposed to a contractor, for example) can be complicated. Again, if you are unsure about whether you are subject to the regulations, it's best to contact one of the EEOC's field offices (or your attorney) to get help with evaluating applicability. (Please see the URL listed just above for finding the appropriate field office.)

3) VARIOUS DEPARTMENTS AND AGENCIES WITHIN THE INDIVIDUAL STATE AND LOCAL GOVERNMENTS

Despite the Department of Labor and Equal Opportunities Employment Commission regulations, currently no national-level Domestic Workers' Bill of Rights exists. In recent years, domestic worker rights advocates have pursued a grassroots campaign to gain further protections for household employees. Their efforts resulted in New York's Governor signing the Domestic Workers' Bill of Rights and, on November 29, 2010, NY became the first state to enact a law providing a Domestic Workers' Bill of Rights. The legislation is designed to provide basic labor protections to household workers (additional details on NY's bill of rights are provided below). The second state to sign into law basic protections for domestic workers was Hawaii in July of 2013. California became the third state to enact similar legislation, and the law took effect in January of 2014.

Since many of our clients have a primary or secondary residence in New York State, I'll provide NYS regulatory information as a state-level example. (Note that while additional local regulations apply within various parts of NY state, I will focus only on state-level laws.) As mentioned, in 2010, New York enacted a Domestic Workers' Bill of Rights. This law provides household workers with an eight-hour workday and overtime (at time-and-a-half) for working over 40 hours per week (or 44 hours if the employee lives on their employer's property). Additionally, the law requires that household employees must be granted one twenty-four-hour-day off every seven days of work or be paid overtime if the employee agrees to work on the seventh day. The law also requires that after an employee has worked for one year with an employer, the worker must be granted three paid days off every year.

For more detailed information regarding New York State's domestic employer requirements, please see "Facts for Employers" (from the NY Department of Labor), which can be found at the following URL:

https://labor.ny.gov/legal/laws/pdf/domestic-workers/facts-for-employers.pdf

Below I'll provide a summary of key points from NY's "Facts for Employers" document. The introductory section of the fact sheet entitled "What are your responsibilities under the New York labor law?" provides a brief overview of the requirements for NY domestic employers. To ensure an accurate account of the state's requirements, much of the following information is taken verbatim (or with only slight changes) from the NY Department of Labor's website or fact sheets:

"If you employ one or more domestic workers, you must:

◆ *Pay your worker at least the minimum wage appropriate for your region. See the minimum wage schedule at www.labor.ny.gov/minimumwage. You may need or choose to pay more than the minimum wage. If you provide meals and/or lodging for your employee, you may* receive a credit toward the minimum wage paid to the worker. Call 1-888-52-LABOR for more information.

◆ Pay overtime at 1-1/2 times your employee's basic rate after 40 hours of work in a calendar week. If your employee lives in your home, you must pay overtime after 44 hours of work in a week.

◆ Provide one day (24 hours) of rest per week. If your employee agrees to work on that day, you must pay overtime. The law encourages you to (where possible) set your employee's day of rest to coincide with their day of worship, if they have one.

◆ Give at least three paid days off after one year of work for you. Again, you may provide more than three paid days off.

◆ Offer a written notice about your policies on sick leave, vacation, personal leave, holidays and hours of work.

◆ Give your employee a written notice that lists the regular and overtime rates of pay and the regular payday. You can find a sample on the Department of Labor website (see **https://www.labor.ny.gov/formsdocs/wp/LS54.pdf**).

◆ Not retaliate against a worker(s) for complaining to you or to the Labor Department about labor law violations. See more information about the Department of Labor Division of Labor Standards.

You can get additional information about the Department of Labor Division of Labor Standards (**https://labor.ny.gov/legal/domestic-workers-bill-of-rights.shtm**)."

NY's "Facts for Employers" also provides information about the state's requirements for the following topics:

◆ Required insurance coverage

◆ New human rights protections

- Health insurance
- Other state and federal taxes
- If you hire an immigrant domestic worker

As mentioned, I highly recommend that household employers in New York State read "Facts for Employers," which is available at:

https://labor.ny.gov/legal/laws/pdf/domestic-workers/ facts-for-employers.pdf

to gain a more complete understanding of the state's provisions.

4) THE IRS

Household employers are also legally required to meet federal and state tax obligations. Please see **Appendix III**, which provides information on the IRS's tax requirements for household employers, and speak with your tax advisor.

5) US CITIZENSHIP AND IMMIGRATION SERVICES

The final regulator whose rules household employers are subject to is US Citizenship and Immigration Services. Any employee who works in your home must confirm that they can legally work for you by completing Form I-9, Employment Eligibility Verification.

U.S. Citizenship and Immigration Services (see **https://www. uscis.gov/i-9**) advises the following:

> *"Form I-9 is used for verifying the identity and employment authorization of individuals hired for employment in the United States. All U.S. employers must ensure proper completion of Form I-9 for each individual they hire for employment in the United States. This includes citizens and noncitizens. Both employees and employers (or authorized representatives of the employer) must complete the form."*

A NOTE ON INSURANCE COVERAGE

Another factor to consider as a domestic employer is insurance coverage. Forms of insurance relevant to household employers — in addition to homeowner's and auto insurance — include workers compensation insurance, valuable collections insurance, and umbrella liability insurance. It's wise to have protections in place in the unlikely event that, for example, a household employee is involved in a car accident while driving one of your cars, or the employee is severely injured while on your property. Ideally, residential employees would also have auto and umbrella liability policies to provide additional coverage in the event of an accident. As is the case with legal and tax matters, insurance considerations are best left to the experts in the field, and your own insurance agent is the right person to advise you on the insurance coverage that's appropriate for you.

APPENDIX III.

FEDERAL TAX REQUIREMENTS FOR HOUSEHOLD EMPLOYERS

Household employers often have questions about tax considerations related to domestic staff employment, and for good reason. When domestic employers do not properly classify employees and the employers fail to make the required tax filings and payments, the IRS may consider this tax fraud. In this chapter, we'll focus on U.S. federal tax requirements only, as a state-by-state overview is beyond the scope of this book. However, it must be noted that state requirements should not be overlooked, as penalties and interest assessed by the various state taxation departments could be substantial.

I would also like to point out that while my fellow Rotarian, John Larkin, CPA, ABV, of Markowitz, Fenelon & Bank, LLP in Bridgehampton, NY (see **http://www.mfbcpa.com**) kindly advised on this appendix, every household employer's situation is unique, and it's wise to consult a tax professional to discuss your particular household situation. Moreover, given the complexity of domestic employment tax compliance, you may choose to work with a firm that offers not only advice for household employers, but also household payroll and payroll tax services.

With that said, the right place to start to gain an understanding of federal tax obligations is the seventeen-page "IRS Publication 926, Household Employer's Tax Guide" (see **https://www.irs.gov/pub/irs-pdf/p926.pdf**). The information provided below is excerpted from that guide. I've included certain sections only to offer you a concise, big-picture view of the primary federal tax requirements that affect most domestic employers. Much of the information is quoted word-for-word or with only very minor modifications to most accurately convey the IRS's requirements.

The introduction of the "Household Employer's Tax Guide" notes, "If you have a household employee in 2019, you may need to pay state and federal employment taxes for 2019. You generally must add your federal employment taxes to the income tax that you will report on your 2019 federal income tax return." Moreover, the tax guide can "help you decide whether you have a household employee and, if you do, whether you need to pay federal employment taxes (social security tax, Medicare tax, FUTA, and federal income tax withholding). [The guide] explains how to figure, pay, and report these taxes for your household employee. It also explains what records you need to keep. [The guide] also tells you where to find out whether you need to pay state unemployment tax for your household employee." Below is a summary of core sections of IRS Publication 926.

WHO SHOULD BE CLASSIFIED AS A HOUSEHOLD EMPLOYEE?

The IRS's criteria for whether your household worker should be classified as an employee are relatively straightforward. If you hire someone to work in your private home and you direct that person's work, then the worker is your employee. Here's how the IRS explains it in the tax guide:

> "You have a household employee if you hired someone to do household work and that worker is your employee. The worker is your employee if you can control not only what work is done but how it is done. If the worker is your employee, it doesn't matter whether the work is full time or part time or that you hired the worker through an agency or from a list provided by an agency or association. It also doesn't matter whether you pay the worker on an hourly, daily, or weekly basis, or by the job."

The tax guide provides some helpful examples to consider in deciding whether your domestic worker is an employee. Here's one such example:

> "You pay Betty Shore to babysit your child and do light housework four days a week in your home. Betty follows your specific instructions about household and childcare duties. You provide the household equipment and supplies that Betty needs to do her work. Betty is your household employee."

WHAT WORK IS CLASSIFIED AS HOUSEHOLD WORK? WHAT CATEGORIES OF WORKERS ARE CONSIDERED HOUSEHOLD WORKERS?

The IRS tax guide also offers a definition of what is considered "household work," and which categories of workers are deemed to be household workers. Information on people who may work in your home but who should not be considered household workers is also provided:

Household work is work done in or around your home. Here are some examples of workers who do household work:

◆ Babysitters

◆ Butlers

◆ Caretakers

◆ Cooks

◆ Domestic workers

◆ Drivers

◆ Health aides

◆ Housecleaning workers

◆ Housekeepers

◆ Maids

◆ Nannies

◆ Private nurses and

◆ Yard workers

Household work doesn't include services performed by these workers unless the services are performed in or around your private home. A separate and distinct dwelling unit maintained by you in an apartment house, hotel, or other similar establishment is considered a private home. Services not of a household nature, such as services performed as a private secretary, tutor, or librarian, even though performed in your home, aren't considered household work.

WHO SHOULD NOT BE CLASSIFIED AS A HOUSEHOLD EMPLOYEE?

Now let's take a look at what types of workers are not considered to be your employees by the IRS:

"If only the worker can control how the work is done, the

worker isn't your employee but is self-employed. *A self-employed worker usually provides his or her own tools and offers services to the general public in an independent business. A worker who performs childcare services for you in his or her home generally isn't your employee. If an agency provides the worker and controls what work is done and how it is done, the worker isn't your employee.*"

Here is an example of a work arrangement in which the worker would not be considered your employee:

"*You made an agreement with John Peters to care for your lawn. John runs a lawn care business and offers his services to the general public. He provides his own tools and supplies, and he hires and pays any helpers he needs. Neither John nor his helpers are your household employees.*"

WHAT ARE YOUR PAYROLL TAX OBLIGATIONS AS A HOUSEHOLD EMPLOYER?

Once you have determined if you have a household employee, and you pay that household worker $2,100 or more (for 2019), then you are responsible for employment taxes, including all Social Security and Medicare taxes. You'll also need to pay federal unemployment taxes for funding unemployment. In the "Do You Need To Pay Employment Taxes?" section of the tax guide, the IRS offers the following guidance:

"*If you have a household employee, you may need to withhold and pay social security and Medicare taxes, pay federal unemployment tax, or both.*" *A brief and clear table, which can help you to determine your obligations and which I encourage you to review, is provided in the online PDF version of the tax guide: Table 1. Do You Need To Pay Employment Taxes? (Please see the table below or page four of* **https://www.irs.gov/pub/irs-pdf/p926.pdf**.)

Table 1. **Do You Need To Pay Employment Taxes?**

IF you ...	THEN you need to ...
A Pay cash wages of $2,100 or more in 2019 to any one household employee. Don't count wages you pay to: • Your spouse, • Your child under the age of 21, • Your parent (see Wages not counted, later, for an exception), or • Any employee under the age of 18 at any time in 2019 (see Wages not counted, later, for an exception).	Withhold and pay social security and Medicare taxes. • The taxes are 15.3%[1] of cash wages. • Your employee's share is 7.65%.[1] (You can choose to pay it yourself and not withhold it.) • Your share is 7.65%.
B Pay total cash wages of $1,000 or more in any calendar quarter of 2018 or 2019 to household employees. Don't count wages you pay to: • Your spouse, • Your child under the age of 21, or • Your parent.	Pay federal unemployment tax. • The tax is 6% of cash wages. • Wages over $7,000 a year per employee aren't taxed. • You also may owe state unemployment tax.

Source: IRS

The IRS stipulates the following:

"You don't need to withhold federal income tax from your household employee's wages. But if your employee asks you to withhold it, you can. The employee must give you a completed Form W-4. If you and your employee have agreed to withholding, either of you may end the agreement by letting the other know in writing. If you agree to withhold federal income tax, you're responsible for paying it to the IRS."

For more information, review "Do You Need To Withhold Federal Income Tax" on page 8 of the tax guide at **https://www.irs.gov/pub/irs-pdf/p926.pdf**. Keep in mind that it is considered to be standard practice to deduct income taxes from your household employee's wages to help prevent a situation in which your employee owes a substantial amount of money when they file their taxes. If an employee elects not to withhold federal withholding taxes, I would suggest obtaining the employee's election in order to avoid a problem when, later, the employee files their personal taxes.

If you do need to pay social security, Medicare, or federal unemployment tax or choose to withhold federal income tax, read Table 2, the Household Employer's Checklist, which is provided below and on page 5 of IRS Publication 926. In particular, Table 2 provides guidance on what you may need to do "When you hire a household employee" and "When you pay your household employee."

Table 2. **Household Employer's Checklist**
You may need to do the following things when you have a household employee.

When you hire a household employee:	❑ Find out if the person can legally work in the United States. ❑ Find out if you need to withhold and pay federal taxes. ❑ Find out if you need to withhold and pay state taxes.
When you pay your household employee:	❑ Withhold social security and Medicare taxes. ❑ Withhold federal income tax. ❑ Decide how you will make tax payments. ❑ Keep records.
By January 31, 2020:	❑ Get an employer identification number (EIN). ❑ Give your employee Copies B, C, and 2 of Form W-2, Wage and Tax Statement. ❑ Send Copy A of Form W-2 with Form W-3 to the SSA. Don't send Form W-2 to the SSA if you didn't withhold federal income tax and the social security and Medicare wages were below $2,100 for 2019.
By April 15, 2020:	❑ File Schedule H (Form 1040), Household Employment Taxes, with your 2019 federal income tax return (Form 1040, 1040NR, 1040-SS, or 1041). If you don't have to file a return, file Schedule H by itself.

Source: IRS

The federal employment tax payments you make are reconciled with the information on your employee's income tax return. Keep in mind that you may also need to submit quarterly unemployment tax filings and reports and payments of state income taxes withheld. You are required to provide each employee with their W-2 form by January 31 of each year.

REVIEW THE FULL IRS TAX GUIDE OR SPEAK WITH YOUR ACCOUNTANT ABOUT BOTH FEDERAL AND STATE REQUIREMENTS

The information in this appendix offers but a brief introduction to IRS tax requirements for household employers. As mentioned, I highly recommend that you review the guide used as the basis of this chapter, IRS Publication 926, the "Household Employer's Tax Guide" to gain a fuller understanding of your federal tax obligations. Moreover, as detailed in **Appendix II**, a household employer must determine if an employee is eligible to work legally in the United States. Please see the US Citizenship and Immigration Services website regarding completing a Form I-9, Employment Eligibility Verification (**https://www.uscis.gov/i-9**).

Lastly, I'd like to mention once again that your tax advisor is the best person to advise you on what you need to do to meet not only the federal but also the state tax requirements. A discussion with your tax professional will no doubt help you best navigate through the ins and outs of your unique tax situation. The potential adverse consequences from multiple federal and state agencies in assessing penalties, interest, and withholding taxes could be substantial if the correct process for collecting and reporting is not followed. Moreover, as mentioned in **Appendix II**, it's also wise to have a conversation with your insurance agent prior to hiring a household employee to ensure that the proper insurance coverage is in place.

ABOUT THE AUTHOR

Aleksandra Kardwell is president and founder of Hamptons Employment Agency, Inc. (HEA), an award-winning domestic staffing firm with offices in New York City, Southampton, Boston, and Boca Raton.

A member of The Entrepreneur's Organization (EO), Aleksandra holds a B.A. in Finance and Banking from The School of Management and Banking in Krakow, Poland, and she completed Columbia Business School's Executive Education Program in Personal Leadership and Success.

Aleksandra is actively involved as a volunteer in the Hamptons community. She holds the following leadership positions:

- President-Elect of the Southampton Rotary Club,
- Auction Co-Chair for the Hamptons Heart Ball,
- Committee member for the St. Jude's "Hope in the Hamptons" event,
- Committee member for the Parrish Art Museum's "Spring Fling," and
- Committee member for the Evelyn Alexander Wildlife Rescue Center's "Get Wild Benefit."

Aleksandra lives on the beautiful East End of Long Island, NY with her husband, daughter, and son. You can contact her by phone at 631-204-1100 or by email at akardwell@ hamptonsemployment.com.

REFERENCES

American Psychological Association (2012). Work-Life Fit and Enjoying What They Do Top the List of Reasons Why Employees Stay On the Job, New APA Survey Finds. Retrieved from https://www.apa.org/news/press/releases/2012/08/work-life.

American Psychological Association (2012). Workplace Survey. Retrieved from: https://www.apa.org/news/press/releases/phwa/workplace-survey.pdf.

Automatic Data Processing, Inc. (ADP) Public Relations (2009, December). Twelfth Annual ADP Screening Index Reveals Nearly 10 Percent of Job Candidates Have Criminal History, Credit Issues or Driving Citations. Retrieved from: http://www.marketwired.com/press-release/twelfth-annual-adp-screening-index-reveals-nearly-10-percent-job-candidates-have-criminal-nasdaq-adp-1179160.htm.

Feiner, Michael (2004). The Feiner Points of Leadership: The 50 Basic Laws That Will Make People Want to Perform Better for You. New York, NY: Warner Business Books.

Gallup (2017). State of the American Workplace. Washington, D.C.

Gallup (2017). What Star Employees Want. Washington, D.C.

Glassdoor (2017). Why Do Workers Quit? Mill Valley, California.

Half, Robert (1985). Robert Half on Hiring. New York, NY: Penguin Group.

Harvard Business Review (2003). Hiring and Keeping the Best People. Boston, MA: Harvard Business Review Press.

Harvard Business Review (2008). Hiring an Employee. Boston, MA: Harvard Business Review Press.

Harvard Business Review (2014). Giving Effective Feedback. Boston, MA: Harvard Business Review Press.

Harvard Business Review. Your New Hires Won't Succeed Unless You Onboard Them Properly. Retrieved from https://hbr.org/2017/06/your-new-hires-wont-succeed-unless-you-onboard-them-properly.

HireRight, LLC (2018, April). 2018 Employment Screening Benchmark Report. Retrieved from: https://www.hireright.com/resources/view/2018-employment-screening-benchmark-report.

Internal Revenue Service. IRS Publication 926, Household Employer's Tax Guide. Retrieved from: https://www.irs.gov/pub/irs-pdf/p926.pdf.

Lynn, Adele (2008). The EQ Interview: Finding Employees with High Emotional Intelligence. New York, NY: AMACOM.

New York State Department of Labor. Facts for Employers. Retrieved March 2019 from: https://labor.ny.gov/legal/laws/pdf/domestic-workers/facts-for-employers.pdf.

Robinson, Adam (2017). The Best Team Wins. Austin, TX: Greenleaf Book Group Press.

Society for Human Resource Management (2016). SHRM's 2016 Employee Job Satisfaction and Engagement: The Doors of Opportunity are Open research report. Retrieved from: https://www.shrm.org/hr-today/trends-and-forecasting/research-and-surveys/Documents/2017-Employee-Job-Satisfaction-and-Engagement-Executive-Summary.pdf.

The U.S. Equal Employment Opportunity Commission. Employers. Retrieved March 2019 from: https://www.eeoc.gov/employers.

Tracey, J.B. and Hinkin, T.R. (2006). The Costs of Employee Turnover: When the Devil Is in the Details. Center for Hospitality Research Publications, Cornell University. Retrieved from: https://scholarship.sha.cornell.edu/cgi/viewcontent.cgi?referer=&httpsredir=1&article=1148&context=chrpubs.

Troedson, Maggie (2017, December). This Is How Many People Are Lying on Their Resumes. Retrieved from: https://about.udemy.com/news/this-is-how-many-people-are-lying-on-their-resumes.

U.S. Citizenship and Immigration Services. I-9, Employment Eligibility Verification. Retrieved April 2019 from https://www.uscis.gov/i-9.

United States Department of Labor. Home Care: Domestic Service Final Rule Frequently Asked Questions (FAQs). Retrieved March 2019 from: https://www.dol.gov/whd/homecare/faq.htm.

Wharton@Work (2016, October). Onboarding Best Practices: Create Maximum Value from External Hires. Retrieved from: https://executiveeducation.wharton.upenn.edu/thought-leadership/wharton-at-work/2016/10/onboarding-best-practices.

WorldatWork (2019). WorldatWork 2018-2019 Salary Budget Survey: Top-Level Results. Retrieved from: https://worldatwork.org/docs/research-and-surveys/sbs/SBS2018_19_TopLevelData_NonParticipants.pdf.

INDEX

discrimination, employee
protection against, 113–15
disqualifiers
candidate misrepresentation, 13
elimination factors in applicant
profile, 58
interviews, fabrications and lies
told during, 40
red flags, 37, 38, 62
Domestic Couples, job description
and salary range, 95–96
domestic experience
job descriptions, clearly defining
expectations in, 21, 89
overqualified candidates, 24, 37,
48
past related-job success and,
18–19
scattered experience, resume
file-names indicating, 37
situational interview questions
for less-experienced
candidates, 44
domestic placement specialists
agency assessment, 30–31
benefits of using, 19–20, 30
job descriptions, principals
providing agencies with, 23
private event staffing, as a
service of, 106
property walk-through with
agents as recommended, 48
domestic staff
domestic workers, categorized
as, 111
experience requirements,
reconsidering, 23–24
FLSA, protected by, 109–12
household employees, classified
as, 124–25
natural service-orientation as a
plus, 40
non-disclosure agreements as a
must, 64
onboarding process for new
hires, 65–67
perks and benefits, 87
trial period, payment for time
spent in, 60

See also individual job titles
Domestic Workers Bill of Rights,
115–16

E

East Hampton Star (newspaper), 27
elder care, 28, 96, 104–6, 109
email
email-based reference checks,
51
job description, providing in
email, 26
non-hires, contacting through,
47
thank-you messages, sending
via, 87
welcome email, sending after
job offer, 61
employee recruitment
domestic staffing agencies,
working with, 30–31
friends and associates,
obtaining referrals from,
29–30
newspaper ads, running, 26–27
online job posting, 27–29
recruitment costs of high
employee turnover, 72
three core factors in
recruitment, 25
employee retention, 76, 77–80, 90
employee salaries
annual salary increases, 85–86
first-year salaries, agencies
charging percentage of, 72
job retention, salary as a factor
in, 76
newspaper ads, supplying salary
information to, 26
red flag compensation requests,
61–62
welcome letters, salaries
confirmed in, 63
See also individual job titles
employee turnover
costs associated with, 71–74
employee retention, factors in,
14, 65, 75–76

overtime pay requirements
exemptions from, 109–10
FLSA wage rules, 111, 112
in New York state, 116, 117

P

Personal Assistants (PAs), 103
Personal Care Aides (PCAs), 92–93,
105, 111
position descriptions
checklist, 21
interviews, keeping descriptions
on hand during, 23
preliminary questions, gaining
clarity on job through, 16
principals providing, 25–26
sales element, applying to job
description, 27
private event staffing, 106

R

record-keeping requirements,
111–12
recruitment. *See* employee
recruitment
red flags, 37, 38, 62
references
additional references,
requesting at secondary
interview, 59
reference letters, confirming by
phone call, 49
right questions, verifying
references with, 13
strong candidates, checking
references of, 47
suggested verification questions,
50
resume screening
inaccuracies, taking into
account, 35–36
reading between the lines, 13
red flags, 37, 38, 62
Robert Half on Hiring (Half), 16, 25, 39
Robinson, Adam, 17–18
Russell, Steven T., 108

S

salaries. *See* employee salaries
SARAH feedback model, 83–84
Security Guards, job description
and salary range, 103–4
Senior Care Aides, job description
and salary range, 104–6
SentryLink screening services,
54–55
Social Security Numbers (SSNs), 54,
55, 112
Social Security taxes, 122, 125, 127
Southampton Press (newspaper), 27

T

tax compliance
Household Employer's Tax
Guide, 122, 128
household workers, defining for
tax purposes, 123–25
payroll tax obligations, 125–28
state tax laws, variability in, 62
trial periods, 31, 59–61
turnover. *See* employee turnover

U

Udemy survey on resume lies, 36
United States citizen and
immigration services, 108,
118, 128

W

welcome letters, 61, 63–64
Wharton School onboarding
guidelines, 65–67
Workforce Retention Survey
findings, 77–78

CPSIA information can be obtained
at www.ICGtesting.com
Printed in the USA
BVHW060131180619
551090BV00001B/1/P